Chae

KOREAN SLOW FOOD
FOR A BETTER LIFE

Chae

JUNG EUN CHAE

Hardie Grant

BOOKS

INTRODUCTION
7

SPECIALTY INGREDIENTS AND EQUIPMENT
18

HOW TO USE THIS BOOK
27

ESSENTIAL FERMENTED INGREDIENTS
29

SUMMER
59

AUTUMN
107

WINTER
154

SPRING
209

INDEX
246

ACKNOWLEDGEMENTS
253

ABOUT THE AUTHOR
254

INTRODUCTION

My story is a slow and quiet one. It's about tradition and change, connection and absence, and a refusal to let go of impossible dreams. When I was a child, traditional Korean food seemed to be a burden, carried through the seasons and years by my mother, who was always working, busy preparing food from fresh ingredients. I helped her, but from a sense of duty not a feeling of pleasure.

But just as kimchi and soy sauce mature over time, I have transformed and changed, too. A move to Australia, a brush with adversity and the miracle of happenstance led to an altered perspective.

I now see these Korean traditions as a joy, and I am honoured to be a custodian of methods and recipes that anchor me in time, place and culture, and allow me to share food that is healthy, delicious and interesting. My story is dual and also seamless. It's about Chae the person and CHAE the restaurant. Where one starts and the other begins, I am not always sure.

TRADITION AS DUTY

I was born in Seoul. My father was a policeman and my mother was from farming people in Jeollanam-do, the southernmost region of Korea. Her town Haenam is often called 'ddang-kkeut maeul' or 'village at the end of the earth'. She cared for me, her only child, but as she was the first daughter of her family of seven children, she had a responsibility to take care of her siblings and parents, too.

A key childhood memory is my mum making huge batches of kimchi every winter to share with her brothers and sisters, and my father's family. We would return to Jeollanam-do and neighbours would gather to prepare with us. Once the kimchi was made and distributed locally, my father would pack 20 kilograms (45 lb) of kimchi into thick plastic bags and prepare a delivery box for his family. I remember him taking it to the post office every winter. There were other projects throughout the year: my mother prepared soy sauce and soybean paste, even sesame oil. She grows sesame, collects the sesame seeds, roasts them and presses them in a communal press.

Does it sound idyllic? We didn't see it like that at the time. My mother always said that she hated cooking. It was just what she had to do. Korea was, until recently, a very poor country. In the old days, people didn't see any romance in the seemingly endless cycles of food preparation and preservation. It was simply about survival. I could see how much it took from my mum. She would be so tired and, every year after the enormous effort of making kimchi, she would get sick for five days. Honestly, I wanted her to stop doing it. It made me angry. And that's why I started helping, out of duty, and because my mum was having such a tough time.

It's only in hindsight that I realised I was fortunate to grow up embedded in these food traditions. Even in Korea, fewer people are making their own preserves and condiments because store-bought items offer more convenient alternatives, and people simply don't have the time in such a fast-paced society. But it took moving to Australia to start to value what was normal in my family. Taste led me there. In Melbourne, I had commercial soybean paste, soy sauce, chilli paste and sesame oil for the first time. I was really shocked. The flavour was nowhere near as nice. I called my mum and she started sending food packages. (My parents have a good relationship with the post office!)

THE ROAD TO AUSTRALIA

It's true that I grew up doing a lot with food, but the idea of a career in cooking didn't occur to me. I studied art from when I was little and my ambition was to be an animator – I love manga. The only problem is, I'm not very talented at art. I entered university but I couldn't really enjoy it and I lost my passion. I was considering the public service exam but my heart wasn't in it and I knew how competitive it was. Korea can be a very high-pressure society when it comes to education and career success. I needed a way out.

A friend was going to Japan to study and it opened my mind to the idea of travel. It wasn't too hard to get a student visa for Australia. I wanted to study something new, so I chose pastry at William Angliss, a hospitality college in Melbourne. I soon realised that pastry wasn't my thing, but as soon as I swapped to regular culinary cookery, I loved it. I was so happy to learn everything. I was curious. I loved to meet chefs to talk about food. I loved to see people enjoying my food. I fell in love with cooking.

I had no English when I arrived. I couldn't even order a coffee. But fluent conversation wasn't too important for an entry-level chef. I learnt enough English to understand instructions. My first job was at a new-style city pub: it was great fun for a first job. Everyone was nice and I learned so many things. Next, I worked at a French brasserie where I was really inspired by the simplicity of an omelette. The chef opened my eyes: you don't need fancy ingredients to make something amazing. I kept moving and learning, working at various restaurants, happy to learn and contribute.

A CRISIS

The culmination of my working life as a chef was a position at Cutler & Co, one of Melbourne's best fine-dining restaurants. I was proud, passionate and energised. Every three months, I moved to a new position in the restaurant, so I was always learning. I loved working and spent as much time there as I could. I couldn't get enough of seeing people enjoying the food that we created for them.

I got to work by motorbike and one morning someone hit me from behind, injuring my ankle. Determined to continue with my job, I returned to Cutler & Co as soon as I felt able. However, working in a restaurant demands long hours of standing and often involves strenuous physical labour. Unfortunately, my injured ankle wasn't strong enough to meet the job's demands. I held on to my dream job for as long as I possibly could, but eventually I had to come to terms with the fact that I was no longer physically able to perform my role on the team. I vividly remember the tears I shed when I left because I had devoted so much time and effort to pursuing a career in the fine-dining scene, and suddenly, I found myself adrift without a clear sense of direction.

A CHANGE IN DIRECTION

I was feeling very down and uncertain. What could I do? I looked at aged care as a possibility and investigated courses to retrain. One night, I was watching TV and I saw the Netflix *Chef's Table* episode with Buddhist nun Jeong Kwan. I cried. I was so moved, and inspired by her philosophy, her connection to nature. Within a week, I flew to Korea, went to her temple, and asked her if I could work with her. I was nervous but she said yes!

I worked at the temple for two months. People come there to experience temple food – there's a big restaurant there. My job was to prepare food for the guests and workshops, to clean, to wash dishes. People come from all over the world to work with Jeong Kwan. There are rooms for staff so you can stay on-site. After the temple, I went to stay with my mum for two months. I helped her make so much kimchi and chilli paste, but this time it felt different. It wasn't a chore anymore. I was so happy. I realised my real master is my mum. Even though Jeong Kwan was inspiring and motivational, I discovered that as long as you have the mindset to learn, you can learn from anyone. And for me, anyone is my mum, who has been with me my entire life.

A BUBBLING IDEA

I'd had a concept in the back of my mind ever since I started cooking. Now it bubbled to the surface again. I dreamed of a restaurant with just one table. The idea lingered in my mind and would not go away. Whenever I spoke about it with friends or family, they always said it wasn't possible, you couldn't make money like that, you have to be rich first, then you can do it. Even my husband Yoora said this. But I wanted to try; I couldn't let the idea go.

Now was the time. I couldn't work in the way that I had. Yoora had a full-time job with a steady income, so it wasn't too risky. It seemed like it was meant to be. It was a time of juggling ideas. No one thought it was going to succeed but we could at least try the concept.

CHAE BEGINS

I started very small, with a makgeolli (cloudy rice wine) workshop and lunch for just two people in our apartment in Brunswick, a northern suburb of Melbourne. The first visit was November 2019. Word travelled quite fast. People found the concept unique and the idea of going into someone's apartment to try Korean food and learn how to make makgeolli and also kimchi was very appealing. Bookings came in steadily via Instagram messages and we were soon doing three lunches a week.

We found ourselves quite lucky, in a way, because it was during the midst of the pandemic when people were actively avoiding crowded places, and the interest in healthy eating and organic fermentation had never been higher. Additionally, Korean cuisine was steadily gaining recognition, thanks to the global spread of Korean pop culture and movies. We soon realised people were more interested in eating than making, so we stopped the workshops and started thinking that one day we might do a book to share that knowledge.

Chae is quite a unique family name in Korea, and I always knew I would use it for my restaurant. Once I started my fledgling business, I needed a logo for my website and social media. I turned to Yoora for help, as he was working as a fashion designer back then and had a good eye for design. However, he wasn't overly excited about my humble business plan and he procrastinated. Eventually he designed our logo in one minute, writing 'Chae' in Korean and styling it to resemble a traditional stamp. Luckily, it's good! The design grows on you, and I am still using the same logo to this day.

In the height of the pandemic, Victoria was known as one of the toughest states in Australia when it came to preventative lockdowns and restrictions. Many businesses were going through tough times, having to repeatedly open and close at limited capacity. I was no exception. Apart from having to close the business during lockdown, cancelling and rearranging bookings involved disappointment and extra effort, but it gave us time to refine our ideas and progress our offering. Through trial and error, we realised the ideal number of guests was six at a time, served over two lunches and two dinners a week. Any more and it wasn't possible to prepare my style of food – dependent on fermentation and traditional Korean preparations – and deliver a personalised, tailored service to each guest.

CHAE GROWS

In the age of social media, information spreads rapidly without the necessity for large-scale campaigns supported by major corporations. The unique concept of CHAE and my traditional cooking style quickly gained the interest of enthusiasts, eventually capturing the attention of Pat Nourse, the renowned food writer and Creative Director of the Melbourne Food and Wine Festival. He shared news of what we were doing and, suddenly, we garnered attention from various publications and news outlets. Following Pat's discovery, numerous writers, reviewers and critics visited CHAE, leading to many accolades, including the prestigious recognition of two hats in the 2023 and 2024 *Good Food Guide*. I don't often get too emotional, but being included alongside my culinary heroes and the restaurants I've admired since entering the industry was an absolute honour and privilege.

As soon as we opened the booking calendar, the seats for the next month would book out in less than one minute. At one point, we had a wait list of 10,000 a month. And we only served 100 customers a month in total! We frequently received numerous email enquiries and complaints about our website's inaccessibility and bookings being unavailable so quickly. We realised that the conventional reservation system was not sustainable and we had to do something to improve it. We didn't want anyone to be deterred from trying to experience our restaurant.

Yoora pitched a brilliant idea of using a random lottery system for bookings. The idea is quite simple. We open our booking calendar for three weeks, during which people can select their preferred date and party size at their leisure. We gather all the entries, and on the first Monday of every month, we randomly select our guests from the pool of lottery participants. We even share the selection process live on our social media, ensuring that everyone has an equal chance of booking and making the process transparent for all.

I never imagined there would be this level of enthusiasm around my humble home-based restaurant and also authentic Korean cuisine in general. I was happy, but I tried not to think about the external buzz too much. In reality, it's this service that is important: the next lunch, the next dinner. My thoughts were all turned to making each guest happy. I just tried to do my best.

For the first two years, Yoora kept working as a menswear designer. CHAE was getting a lot of attention, but it wasn't making money. Yoora worked regular hours for a steady income, and after hours he did the grocery shopping and the cleaning. In 2022, he quit and we both started working full time on the restaurant and the brand. I have a feeling there will be a day Yoora will be able to bring his fashion talents into CHAE.

It's a good balance. Yoora is good with brand and business. I am purely kitchen. Sometimes we joke about ourselves like the legendary Apple team. I am Steve Wozniak, the geeky engineer. Yoora is more Steve Jobs, the vision, design, perception.

As CHAE gained more attention and interest, the demand for additional storage space for my ever-increasing ferments became evident. We also had to factor in our budget, which prompted us to explore more affordable regional areas outside the city. Additionally, we believed that the tranquil and serene hillside setting of Cockatoo, east of Melbourne, aligned perfectly with my culinary philosophy and approach.

Since the move, we strongly feel that coming to this beautiful region was the right decision. This location allows us to offer a truly unique dining experience for our guests, providing an escape from the hustle and bustle of daily life. The spacious outdoor area has given us the opportunity to import oongi from Korea, the traditional clay jars used to store ferments.

Making in-house condiments from scratch, especially storing them in these traditional vessels, has always been considered challenging and financially impractical in the commercial space due to the large area and lengthy preparation time required, making it difficult to generate immediate revenue. Thanks to our unique setup in the spacious hills, we feel extremely privileged to be one of the very few, if not the only, venue in Australia capable of creating our own Korean flavours using traditional methods and techniques.

I'm often asked about what's next on the horizon for CHAE. I've always wanted to create a unique space where I could tune out all the inevitable noise associated with running a conventional restaurant, such as managing staff and the pressure of turning enough profit to cover expensive overheads. At CHAE, I can solely focus on cooking, delivering a high-quality dining experience and engaging with my customers in a very intimate setting.

I'm not planning on expanding the restaurant, because it's a setup I am most comfortable with, and this is what people appreciate and come to CHAE to experience. However, I often feel disappointed that my intimate setup with limited accessibility makes it difficult to engage with a larger audience. For this reason, I actively turn to social media and writing books and blogs as alternative channels for communicating with our followers and sharing our culture through food with them.

This book is a great start, and I feel heartfelt gratitude for my publisher, Hardie Grant, for allowing this opportunity. Finally, I'd like to take this opportunity to express my sincere gratitude for everyone who shows interest and support in what we do, and in Korean cuisine and culture in general. Melbourne has such a dynamic food scene, and I feel very lucky to be able to share the lesser-known aspects of Korean cuisine with our audience.

SPECIALTY INGREDIENTS
AND EQUIPMENT

INGREDIENTS

Most specialty ingredients are available from Korean or Asian grocers, both in store and online.

ACORN POWDER
A powder that can be hydrated to form acorn jelly. You may see it labelled dotorimuk garu.

AEKJEOT (FISH SAUCE)
Korean fish sauce is usually made from anchovies, salted and left to ferment, then strained.

SEA SALT
The traditional way of making nigari or bittern, the magnesium-rich coagulant that's used to make tofu, is by harvesting fresh sea salt. Seawater is slowly drained from salt to create bittern and the salt remaining can be considered bittern-removed.

CHEONGJU
A clear, filtered Korean rice wine.

JUJUBE
A dried red fruit, sometimes known as Chinese red date.

DRIED KELP AND OTHER SEAWEED
Seaweed is a common ingredient in broths and stocks.

ANCHOVY & KELP BROTH

Myeolchi Dasima yuksoo 멸치 다시마 육수

MAKES 2 LITRES (68 FL OZ/8 CUPS)

Broth is a universal ingredient in many types of cooking, and Korean cuisine is no exception. Whether you're preparing a spicy stew with aged tangy kimchi, or delicately seasoned herbs to accompany a bowl of rice, broth acts as a blank canvas that can be tailored to suit your culinary needs. In this book, anchovy and kelp broth is widely used as a base for many recipes.

5 × 5 cm (2 × 2 in) piece of dried kelp
15 g (½ oz/½ cup) dried anchovies

Place the kelp and anchovies in a saucepan with 2 litres (68 fl oz/8 cups) water and bring to the boil over a high heat. Reduce the heat and simmer for about 15 minutes.

Remove the solids and store the broth in an airtight container in the fridge for up to 3 days.

Acorn jelly

FERMENTED FRUIT EXTRACT

Balhyo-aek 발효액

MAKES 800–900 ML (27–30½ FL OZ)

This extract is made by picking seasonal fruits (or vegetables) when they're at their nutritional peak and combining them with sugar, which comprises 80 per cent of the total fruit weight. As the sugar slowly liquefies over time, it draws out the nutritional essence from the ingredients through osmosis, infusing it into the sugary liquid. Once this process is complete, and the flavour is fully infused, we separate the resulting liquid, or extract, which in Korean is referred to as 'cheong'. This extract is carefully stored and reserved for future use in cooking. Traditionally, it is made with pears or plums, but you can replace the pears with any fruit or vegetable that you like.

1 tablespoon bicarbonate of soda (baking soda)
1 kg (2 lb 3 oz) nashi pears, cored
800 g (1 lb 12 oz) raw (demerara) sugar

Combine the bicarbonate of soda with 2 litres (68 fl oz/8 cups) water.

Add the pears to the water and soak for about 5 minutes, then rinse under cold running water and pat dry with paper towel. Lay the pears on a tablecloth and leave to dry completely (if any moisture remains, mould can form).

Sterilise a 5 litre (169 fl oz) wide-mouthed jar (see Tip, page 44), then dry completely.

Quarter the dry pears and ensure all the seeds are removed, then cut the pears into thin slices.

Place one-third of the sugar in the bottom of the jar and place half the sliced pear on top. Add another one-third of the sugar, followed by the remaining sliced pear. Cover the pear with the remaining sugar, then top with a piece of muslin (cheesecloth).

Set the jar aside at room temperature for 10 days, giving the pear a mix at least once a day with clean hands to prevent mould forming.

After 10 days, mould will not form even when it is left unmixed. Leave to ferment for 90 days in a cool, dark place. Once fermented, strain the mixture through a sieve, reserving the pulp (see Tips, below), and store the fruit extract in a bottle at room temperature for up to 1 year.

TIPS

The extract can be used in place of sugar or oligosaccharide for cooking, and it can be mixed with water for drinking.

The remaining pear pulp can be used to make kimchi, or it can be added to the All-purpose soy sauce on page 44.

You can make other fruit or vegetable extracts using this same method.

GOCHUJANG
Korean red chilli paste made with fermented rice flour, soybean powder and gochugaru.

GOCHUGARU
This Korean red chilli powder is warm in colour and flavour and is not overly spicy.

GLUTINOUS RICE FLOUR
Derived from sticky or sweet rice, glutinous rice flour becomes sweet and sticky when hydrated.

JOCHEONG (RICE SYRUP)
Glossy Korean rice syrup used as a sweetener and sugar substitute in recipes.

Jocheong (rice syrup)

GLUTINOUS RICE PASTE

Chapssal juk 찹쌀죽

MAKES APPROX. 2 LITRES (68 FL OZ/8 CUPS)

Glutinous rice paste is one of the foundational ingredients in various kimchi recipes, as it provides the ideal thickness and texture for the seasoning while also supplying the necessary sugar for the fermentation process. In Korean cuisine, it's common practice to prepare glutinous rice paste in large quantities, divide it into portions, and store it in the freezer for future use. Here's a recipe for making your own glutinous rice paste. Enjoy the convenience of having it readily available when you need it.

2 × 10 × 10 cm (4 × 4 in) pieces of dried kelp
15 g (½ oz/½ cup) dried anchovies
15 g (½ oz/½ cup) dried shrimp
80 g (2¾ oz) glutinous rice flour

Combine the kelp, anchovies and shrimp with 2 litres (68 fl oz/8 cups) water in a saucepan. Bring to the boil over a high heat, then reduce the heat to low and simmer for about 15 minutes.

Strain through a fine-mesh sieve into a clean saucepan, discarding the solids. Leave to cool.

Add the glutinous rice flour to the cooled broth and mix well. Stir over a low heat for 20 minutes until the mixture thickens to a paste-like texture. Mix well to prevent any lumps forming.

Remove from the heat and set aside to cool completely. Use the required amount of paste for your recipe, and any remaining paste can be stored in the fridge for up to 3 days in an airtight container, or in the freezer for up to 1 month.

GUKGANJANG (SOUP SOY SAUCE)
A light, salty type of Korean soy sauce that's also called 'soup soy sauce'.

KOREAN RICE WINE
Various beverages are made from rice, including cheongju, makgeolli and soju. Soju can be made from other grains and starches.

JEOTGAL (SALTED SEAFOOD)
A traditional Korean fermented condiment added to many dishes.

MAKGEOLLI
An unfiltered, fermented cloudy rice wine.

PERILLA
A refreshing herb in the mint family, perilla is very popular in Korea. The leaves are commonly made into kimchi, oil is used as a flavouring and dressing, and perilla powder is used in seasonings.

ROASTED SEAWEED
Also called gim (kim). A type of seaweed that's often roasted and crushed for recipes or toppings.

SOJU
A distilled alcoholic beverage, usually made with rice but also with tapioca, sweet potato and barley.

Perilla leaves

EQUIPMENT

BINGSU MACHINE (ICE SHAVER)
Machine for making ice flakes to create bingsu, Korean ice desserts, or for making shaved ice for drinks.

COOKING THERMOMETER
We use a meat thermometer that has a probe and a timer.

DEHYDRATOR
An electric food dehydrator. We layer it with silicone dehydrator sheets for ease of cleaning.

DRIED RICE STRAW
Available from farms, pet stores and livestock supply stores. Ensure it's unsprayed.

FERMENTER
At its most basic, a fermenter can be a food-grade plastic bucket with a lid. Look for them at craft brew supply stores.

FRUIT MESH BAG
Also known as vegetable bags, these are breathable drawstring bags for shopping and storage of fruits and vegetables.

HEMP FIBRE POUCH
A small drawstring bag made of hemp fibre, which is generally foodsafe. Purchase online from craft stores.

MEASURING CUPS
This book uses 250 ml (8½ fl oz) cup measurements. In the US, a cup is 8 fl oz (240 ml), just smaller, so American cooks should be generous in their cup measurements; in the UK, a cup is 9½ fl oz (284 ml), so British cooks should be scant with their cup measurements.

MEJU TRAY MOULD
We have moulds that are specifically designed to shape meju, but you can use any small rectangular container.

MINI GREENHOUSE
Usually used for seedlings, this is a portable and demountable gardening tent with a PVC cover and misting outlets. Available from garden supply stores.

MUSLIN (CHEESECLOTH)
Very fine, food-safe cloth that can be used for straining solids.

ONGGI
A traditional Korean earthenware jar used for fermenting and preserving. The jars are not readily available outside Korea and can be replaced with other fermenters.

ROUND PLASTIC BASIN
16 litre (540 fl oz) basin available at hardware stores. This is ideal for preparing large batches of kimchi.

SEEDLING HEAT PAD
A small electric heating pad used in horticulture for seed propagation. Purchase from hardware and garden supply stores. When combined with a mini greenhouse (see above), a seedling heat pad helps maintain the proper temperature for fermenting.

TABLESPOONS
Please note that this book uses 15 ml (½ fl oz) tablespoons.

TEASPOONS
Please note that this book uses 5 ml (⅛ fl oz) teaspoons.

VACUUM SEALER OR STORAGE BAGS
Plastic bags that are used for sous-vide cooking and food storage. They are used with vacuum machines that remove air from the bag to reduce spoilage or ready it for sous-vide cooking.

WOODEN MIXING PADDLE
Sturdy stirring utensil that is very handy for stirring larger batches of gochujang (Korean red chilli paste) and Fermented fruit extract (page 20). Replace with any spatula.

HOW TO USE
THIS BOOK

When you go deep with Korean food, you make friends with time, you celebrate slowness. That's what I want to show you in this book. The recipes – especially the recipes in the first section, Essential Fermented Ingredients – may seem a little intimidating at first. Some are long, and they require special equipment and a long lead time. We know that. We encourage you to go deep because there really is nothing like making these ingredients from scratch. You will be repaid in flavour and satisfaction. And, more than that, it's not just that your ferments will be delicious, they will be unique to you, to the place and time they were made. They will be healthier, too.

Of course, I understand that for all kinds of reasons not everyone can tackle their own soy sauce. The recipes in this book can be made with store-bought fermented ingredients. I compare it to taking photographs. You can definitely take a great picture with an automatic camera that seamlessly adjusts to the conditions of the day. On the other hand, nothing compares to a manual camera, where you can tweak every detail to make the moment truly yours.

I love living with my ingredients, knowing that they are developing and growing alongside me. I love putting effort and time into them. It makes it so precious: I will not waste a drop of kimchi juice. It connects me with nature and uncertainty, too. I aim for consistency but that calls for sensitivity to variations in produce and weather; responsiveness and flexibility become habits.

I love weaving my years with my ferments and I hope you will too.

TIMELINE OF A DISH

CHICKEN BREAST & CUCUMBER SALAD (PAGE 100)

If you want to prepare all the ferments from scratch for this summer salad, this is your timeline. Don't forget, ingredients you buy are okay, too. In fact, if you start with store-bought, then you will really experience the difference on day 471!

We are making All-purpose soy sauce* (page 44), Fermented fruit extract† (page 20) and Traditional persimmon vinegar◊ (page 55).

DAY 1 (PREFERABLY IN EARLY WINTER)
*Soak the soybeans to begin making the soy sauce.
†Jar the fruit and sugar to begin making the fruit extract.
◊Jar the persimmons to begin making the vinegar.

DAY 2
*Cook and start drying the soybeans to make the meju.

DAY 60
*Soak the meju for 45 days.

DAY 90
†Separate the fruit and sugar to finish the fruit extract.

DAY 105
*Separate the soy and soybean paste, then set aside to age for a year or more.

DAY 150
◊Strain the persimmons.

DAY 330
◊Scoop out and store the persimmon vinegar.

DAY 470
*The soy and soybean paste can be used.

DAY 471
Make your chicken salad!

기본 발효 양념

Gibon balhyo yangnyeom

ESSENTIAL FERMENTED INGREDIENTS

TRADITIONAL KOREAN
SOYBEAN PASTE &
SOUP SOY SAUCE
34

SIMPLIFIED KOREAN
SOYBEAN PASTE &
SOUP SOY SAUCE
40

ALL-PURPOSE SOY SAUCE
44

STICKY FERMENTED
SOYBEAN PASTE
47

GLUTINOUS RICE
RED CHILLI PASTE
48

SALTED SEAFOOD
51

TRADITIONAL PERSIMMON
VINEGAR
55

AUTHENTIC KOREAN CUISINE IS ROOTED IN ITS FERMENTED
CONDIMENTS, WHICH HAVE BEEN PASSED DOWN FROM
GENERATION TO GENERATION. MAKING THESE CONDIMENTS
REQUIRES LONG PREPARATION TIMES, AMPLE STORAGE AND
TRADITIONAL TECHNIQUES, BUT IT IS A VERY REWARDING
PROCESS, AND THE END RESULT IS TRULY WORTH WAITING FOR.

AS SOCIETY HAS MODERNISED AND BECOME MORE FAST-PACED,
THE STORE-BOUGHT ALTERNATIVES HAVE BECOME READILY
AVAILABLE AND, AS A RESULT, THESE TRADITIONALLY PREPARED
CONDIMENTS, WHICH HAVE DEVELOPED ORGANICALLY OVER TIME,
ARE BECOMING INCREASINGLY DIFFICULT TO FIND, EVEN IN KOREA.

I AM OFTEN ASKED WHY I INSIST ON MAKING THESE TRADITIONAL
FERMENTS FROM SCRATCH. IT'S A BIT LIKE USING A MANUAL FILM
CAMERA OVER AN AUTOMATIC DIGITAL ONE. THE DIGITAL ONE
MIGHT PRODUCE A SOPHISTICATED, WELL-CALCULATED RESULT, BUT
IT LEAVES LITTLE ROOM FOR YOUR OWN CREATIVITY, CONTROL AND,
SOMETIMES, THOSE UNEXPECTED 'HAPPY MISTAKES'. STORE-BOUGHT
CONDIMENTS ARE JUST LIKE THIS: THEY ARE PERFECTLY DELICIOUS,
BUT THE FLAVOUR IS UNIFORM AND LACKS YOUR UNIQUE TOUCH.

ON THE OTHER HAND, HOME-MADE TRADITIONAL CONDIMENTS
ALL HAVE THEIR OWN DISTINCT FLAVOUR, AND IT CHANGES YEAR
ON YEAR. MAKING THEM IS A CRAFT THAT REQUIRES INVESTING
CONSTANT CARE AND ATTENTION WHILE YOU AWAIT THE OUTCOME,
MUCH LIKE THE CURIOSITY OF WAITING FOR FILM TO BE DEVELOPED.

IN THIS CHAPTER, I HAVE INCLUDED SOME OF THE BASIC
FERMENTED CONDIMENTS THAT GIVE KOREAN CUISINE ITS
DISTINCTIVE FLAVOUR. I ENCOURAGE YOU TO GIVE THEM A
TRY AND EXPLORE THESE UNIQUE DISHES BY INCORPORATING
THEM INTO YOUR OWN CULINARY CREATIONS.

TRADITIONAL KOREAN SOYBEAN PASTE & SOUP SOY SAUCE

Jaeraesik doenjang & chosun ganjang
재래식 된장 & 조선간장

MAKES 2 LITRES (68 FL OZ/
8 CUPS) SOUP SOY SAUCE
AND 4 KG (8 LB 13 OZ)
SOYBEAN PASTE

Chosun ganjang roughly translates into soup soy sauce, and is a fundamental condiment in various Korean soup dishes. It can also be used beyond soups as a seasoning to enhance a wide range of dishes.

What sets chosun ganjang apart is its distinctive fishy, umami-rich flavour, coupled with its light colour. This unique combination makes it an excellent choice for adding depth to a broth while maintaining the original colour of a dish.

Preparing it can be time consuming (approximately 3 months), which is why we tend to do it in larger batches. This might pose a challenge in smaller households, so if space is limited, you can easily find chosun ganjang at Korean and Asian grocers.

Doenjang is a traditional Korean fermented soybean paste. It is one of the essential ingredients in Korean cuisine, and is incredibly versatile, serving as a base for soups, stews and sauces.

Doenjang and ganjang arise from the same fermentation process. The method involves soaking fermented soybeans in brine to infuse a profound umami flavour into the liquid. The soybeans are then separated, mashed and further aged to develop into the essential Korean condiment. If the lengthy process and space constraints are an issue, store-bought doenjang can be used instead.

Note that you will need a few specialty pieces of equipment for this recipe: empty plastic bottles, rice straw, a dehydrator and a fermenter, see page 24.

2 empty plastic bottles
4 large handfuls of rice straw
4 Meju blocks (see below)
5 litres (169 fl oz) mineral water
1.25 kg (2 lb 12 oz) coarse sea salt
2 dried jujubes, washed well
2 dried chillies
1–2 pieces of hardwood lump
  charcoal
rock salt, for aging

MEJU BLOCKS
2 kg (4 lb 6 oz) soybeans

BOILING MEJU
Start by making the meju blocks. Submerge the soybeans in a bowl of cold water and wash, then drain and rinse. Repeat this process another four times, or until there are no longer any bubbles on the surface of the water.

Place the cleaned soybeans in a deep pot or container and soak in 6 litres (202 fl oz) water for 10 hours, then drain.

Put the soaked soybeans in a large stockpot with 8 litres (270 fl oz) water and bring to the boil over a high heat, skimming any foam that rises to the surface. Once boiling, reduce the heat to medium, partly cover with a lid and boil for 3 hours, stirring with a wooden spoon every hour to ensure the soybeans don't stick to the bottom of the pot.

After 3 hours, reduce the heat to low and almost completely cover the pot with the lid. Simmer for 1 hour. You should be able to crush the beans easily between your fingers. Strain through a fine-mesh sieve, discarding the remaining water.

While the beans are hot, place them in a food processor and blitz to a coarse texture (not too thin).

Place a tea towel (dish towel) in a meju tray mould or a 1.8 litre (61 fl oz) container and stuff it with the mashed beans. Fold the tea towel over the top of the mashed beans and press down firmly to harden and squeeze the air out, then remove from the tea towel. If you've done this correctly, the block should feel firm and heavy.

continued ...

1

2

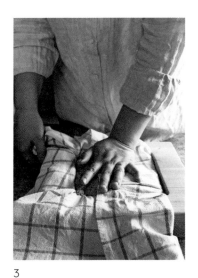

3

4

5

DRYING MEJU

In Korea, meju is made during winter because the cold, dry atmosphere creates the ideal conditions for the right bacteria to grow. If you are making this during the milder Australian winter, we recommend using a dehydrator instead, because the slight humidity and warmer temperatures may cause mould to grow on your meju.

Place the blocks in a dehydrator set to 45°C (113°F) and leave for 20 hours. (We are just trying to dry the outside of the meju here, not the middle of the blocks.)

If you're making meju in a colder environment, like a Korean winter, place your meju blocks on a bamboo mat or bed of dried rice straw and leave in a shaded, well-ventilated place for 3 days to dry.

FERMENTING MEJU

Place each dried meju block in a separate mesh bag with a handful of dried rice straw. Hang the bags in a well-ventilated room and leave at room temperature to ferment for 3 months.

Given this process is conducted in an uncontrolled, open-air space, there are various unexpected factors that can impact the quality of the meju.

The combination of optimal humidity, temperature, oxygen and nutrition will result in the growth of three desirable fungi:

1. *Bacillus subtilis* (white-coloured fungus)
2. *Aspergillus* (ivory-coloured fungus)
3. *Aspergillus oryzae* (pale blue-coloured fungus).

Checking the colour and smell are also common ways to determine if the meju blocks are properly fermented.

Improper conditions can lead to the growth of undesirable fungi. Be on the lookout for fungus colours like grey, black, yellow, blue and red, as they indicate that unwanted bacteria may be growing.

SOAKING MEJU

Clean a 10 litre (338 fl oz) fermenter and dry well, then take a clean cloth and dampen it with food-grade sanitiser. Thoroughly wipe out the fermenter to ensure it is sterilised.

Place each meju block under cold running water and wash, using a soft, clean brush to wipe away any straw, dust or impurities. Lay the washed meju blocks on a clean tea towel and allow to air-dry in a cool, shaded area for 1 day.

Add 5 litres (169 fl oz) mineral water to an 8 litre (270 fl oz) stockpot. Add the salt and stir to dissolve.

Place the meju inside the fermenter and top with two tea towels or clean cloths. Pour the salted water over the top.

The tea towels should filter any impurities in the salt.

Fill the plastic bottles with tap water, then seal. Wipe the bottles with sanitiser, then use them to weigh down the meju blocks inside the fermenter, ensuring they are fully submerged. (If the meju is exposed to air, unwanted mould will grow on the surface.) Alternatively, you can use PET bottles filled with water to hold down the meju.

Add the jujubes, chillies and charcoal on top, which will help to prevent mould forming.

Cover the fermenter with two or three layers of muslin (cheesecloth) and leave in a well-ventilated sheltered area with abundant sunlight. Ferment for 40–45 days. Once a month, change the muslin layers and give the fermenter a good wipe.

SEPARATING SOYBEAN PASTE AND SOY SAUCE
To separate the meju blocks from the brine, remove the jujubes, chillies, charcoal, water bottles and cloths, and place the meju blocks in a large bowl. Pass the fermented brine (aka the soy sauce) through a fine-mesh sieve into another container. You should have about 3 litres (101 fl oz/12 cups) of soy sauce.

Crush the meju blocks well with your hands or with a pestle. Gradually add the 1 litre (34 fl oz/4 cups) of the strained soy sauce, mixing as you go. The consistency should be similar to a cementing paste. If not enough soy sauce is added, the soybean paste will stiffen over time and become dry.

Clean and sterilise the fermenter and return the mashed soybean paste to the fermenter. Press down on top of the mixture to remove any pockets of air. Cover the surface of the paste with a piece of plastic wrap, then top this with a layer of coarse sea salt to prevent mould forming. You can begin using doenjang after a minimum of 1 year of aging. When using doenjang, carefully lift the layer of plastic wrap and sea salt. Scoop the doenjang with a dry spoon, then press down to fill the void. Cover it again with plastic wrap and sea salt. Cover the fermenter with a piece of muslin and store indefinitely in a well-ventilated, sheltered area with abundant sunlight.

Take the remaining 2 litres (68 fl oz/8 cups) soy sauce and pour it into a stockpot. Bring to the boil over a high heat, then remove and allow to cool.

Once the soy sauce is completely cool, pour it into a clean glass jar and cover the opening with a piece of muslin. Leave it in a well-ventilated, sheltered area with abundant sunlight for at least 6 months. The soy sauce will darken in colour as it ages.

Store in a sealed glass jar or bottle indefinitely.

SIMPLIFIED KOREAN SOYBEAN PASTE & SOUP SOY SAUCE

Almeju doenjang & almeju ganjang
알메주 된장 & 알메주 간장

MAKES 2 LITRES (68 FL OZ/
8 CUPS) SOUP SOY SAUCE
AND 4 KG (8 LB 13 OZ)
SOYBEAN PASTE

The key distinction between traditional (see page 34) and simplified doenjang/ganjang lies in their different fermentation techniques and, specifically, the bacteria introduced to ferment the soybeans. In traditional methods, the cooked soybeans are moulded into square shapes, placed in a mesh bag with straw, and hung in an open-air space to facilitate the fermentation of the soybeans by both airborne bacteria and bacteria from the straw. During this process, the soybean blocks are naturally inoculated with various wild bacteria. In contrast, the simplified approach in this recipe creates a controlled environment using tools like mini greenhouses and heating mats to inoculate the soybeans with a single specific strain of bacteria. This simplified approach minimises the risk of the soybeans being inoculated with undesirable bacteria. Additionally, it is not dependent on weather conditions and can be carried out year-round. However, it's worth noting that the flavour may not be as rich and umami as that of traditional doenjang and ganjang.

You will need some equipment for this method: mini greenhouse, seedling heat mat, dehydrator and thermometer (see page 24).

2 empty plastic bottles
4 large handfuls of rice straw
2 kg (4 lb 6 oz) soybeans
5 litres (169 fl oz) mineral water
1.25 kg (2 lb 12 oz) coarse sea
   salt, plus extra for aging the
   soybean paste
2 dried jujubes, washed well
2 dried chillies
1–2 pieces of hardwood lump
   charcoal
rock salt for aging

Submerge the soybeans in a bowl of cold water and wash, then drain and rinse. Repeat this process another four times, or until there are no longer any bubbles on the surface of the water.

Place the cleaned soybeans in a deep pot or container and soak in 5 litres (169 fl oz) water for 10 hours, then drain.

Put the soaked soybeans in a large stockpot with 8 litres (270 fl oz) water and bring to the boil over a high heat, skimming any foam that rises to the surface. Once boiling, reduce the heat to medium, partly cover with a lid and boil for 3 hours, stirring with a wooden spoon every hour to ensure the soybeans don't stick to the bottom of the pot. After 3 hours, reduce the heat to low and almost completely cover the pot with the lid. Simmer for 1 hour. At this point, the beans should be soft enough to crush between your fingers. Strain through a fine-mesh sieve, discarding the remaining water and leave the cooked soybeans to cool down to approximately 25°C (77°F).

Line a metal tray with a clean tea towel (dish towel). Spread the soybeans out in an even layer on the tray. Scatter a handful of rice straw on top and cover with another tea towel.

Place the tray inside the mini greenhouse set on top of the seedling heat mat.

Prepare two thermometers: one to monitor the temperature inside the greenhouse, which should be around 26°C (79°F), and another to be inserted into the soybeans to monitor their temperature, which should be around 30°C (86°F), and no more than 35°C (95°F). Leave to ferment for 3 days.

DRYING FERMENTED SOYBEANS
After 3 days, place a rubber mat or baking tray on a wire-mesh rack and spread the beans out on top. Place in a dehydrator set at 65°C (149°F) for 12 hours until completely dry.

SOAKING THE SOYBEANS
Clean a 10 litre (338 fl oz) fermenter and dry well, then take a clean cloth and dampen it with food-grade sanitiser. Thoroughly wipe out the fermenter to ensure it is sterilised.

Place the dried soybeans in a piece of muslin (cheesecloth) and tie up to create a bag.

Add 5 litres (169 fl oz) mineral water to an 8 litre (270 fl oz) stockpot. Add the sea salt and stir to dissolve.

Place the bag inside the fermenter and top with two tea towels or clean cloths. Pour over the salted water. The tea towels should filter any impurities in the salt.) Fill the plastic bottles with tap water, then seal. Wipe the bottles with sanitiser, then use them to weigh down the meju blocks inside the fermenter, ensuring they are fully submerged. (If the meju is exposed to air, unwanted mould will grow on the surface.) Alternatively, you can use PET bottles, filled with water to hold down the meju. Add the jujubes, chillies and charcoal on top, which will help to prevent mould forming).

Cover the fermenter with two or three layers of muslin and leave in a well-ventilated outdoor area. Ferment for 40–45 days. Once a month, change the muslin layers and give the fermenter a good wipe.

SEPARATING SOYBEAN PASTE AND SOY SAUCE
Remove the tea towels and retrieve the bag of soybeans. Empty the fermented soybeans into a large bowl.

Pass the fermented salted water (aka the soy sauce) through a fine-mesh sieve into a large container. You should have about 3 litres (101 fl oz/12 cups) of soy sauce.

Crush the fermented soybeans well with a pestle. Add the strained soy sauce, starting with 1 litre (34 fl oz/4 cups) and mix well. The consistency should be similar to a cementing paste. If you do not add enough soy sauce, the soybean paste will stiffen over time and become dry, so adjust with a little more soy sauce if needed.

continued ...

Clean and sterilise the fermenter (as described under Soaking the soybeans) and return the mashed soybean paste to the fermenter. Press down on top of the mixture to remove any pockets of air. Cover the surface of the paste with a piece of plastic wrap, then top this with a layer of rock salt to prevent mould forming. You can begin using doenjang after a minimum of 1 year of aging. When using doenjang, carefully lift the layer of plastic wrap and sea salt. Scoop doenjang with a dry spoon, then press down to fill the void. Cover it again with plastic wrap and sea salt. Cover the fermenter with a piece of muslin and store indefinitely in a well-ventilated, sheltered area with abundant sunlight.

Take the remaining 2 litres (68 fl oz/8 cups) of soy sauce and pour it into a stockpot. Heat over a high heat until it comes to the boil, then remove it from the heat and allow to cool.

Once the soy sauce is completely cool, pour it into a clean glass jar and cover the opening with a piece of muslin. Leave it in a well-ventilated outdoor area to age for at least 6 months. The soy sauce will darken in colour as it ages.

Once aged, store in a sealed glass jar or bottle indefinitely.

ALL-PURPOSE SOY SAUCE

Manneung ganjang 만능간장

MAKES APPROX. 2 LITRES
(68 FL OZ/8 CUPS)

As the name suggests, all-purpose soy sauce is the foundational seasoning used in a wide range of dishes in my kitchen. It's a perfect and versatile starting point for crafting seasonings tailored to your specific needs. For this recipe, we use Simplified Korean soup soy sauce (page 40) or Traditional Korean soup soy sauce (page 34) that has been aged for at least 2 years. The colour of this soy sauce deepens as it ages, and due to this darker hue and the complex flavours imparted by various ingredients, it is not ideally suited to seasoning soup dishes or broths.

10 g (¼ oz) dried anchovies

2 litres (68 fl oz/8 cups) Simplified Korean soup soy sauce (page 40) or Traditional Korean soup soy sauce (page 34), aged for at least 2 years

½ apple, quartered and deseeded

½ onion, peeled and halved

2 g (1⁄16 oz) chilli flakes

25 g (1 oz) fresh shiitake mushrooms

1 spring onion (scallion)

5 × 5 cm (2 × 2 in) piece of dried kelp

10 g (¼ oz) piece ginger, peeled

5 garlic cloves, peeled

125 ml (4 fl oz/½ cup) Fermented fruit extract (page 20)

Dry-fry the anchovies in a stockpot over a low heat for 2 minutes.

Add all the remaining ingredients and bring to the boil over a high heat. Once boiling, reduce the heat to medium and simmer for 2 hours, then turn off the heat and allow to cool completely.

Strain through a fine-mesh sieve into a bowl or container, discarding the solids. Store in a sealed sterilised glass bottle (see Tip) in the fridge for up to 2 years.

TIP

To sterilise your bottle, first wash it out with hot soapy water, then dry thoroughly. Dampen a clean cloth with food-grade sanitiser and wipe out the bottle.

1

2

3

4

STICKY FERMENTED SOYBEAN PASTE
Cheonggukjang 청국장

MAKES 2 KG (4 LB 6 OZ)

Cheonggukjang is known for its strong, pungent aroma and robust flavour. The process to make it is very similar to the simplified soybean paste method on page 40. However, the key difference is the fermentation time. When soybeans are inoculated in the controlled settings we've created, they go through different stages of appearance and texture. Initially, they become sticky, producing hair-like, stringy formations. After this, they become drier, and the beans become covered with a snow-like, white, fluffy layer of bacteria. To prepare cheonggukjang, we halt the fermentation process during the sticky, hair-like stage. This results in the distinct characteristics of cheonggukjang, setting it apart from doenjang.

1 kg (2 lb 3 oz) soybeans
1 bundle of rice straw
100 g (3½ oz) coarse sea salt

Submerge the soybeans in a bowl of cold water and wash, then drain and rinse. Repeat this process another four times, or until there are no longer any bubbles on the surface of the water.

Place the cleaned soybeans in a deep pot or container and soak in 3 litres (101 fl oz/12 cups) water for 10 hours, then drain.

Put the soaked soybeans in a large stockpot with 4 litres (135 fl oz/ 16 cups) water and bring to the boil over a high heat, skimming any foam that rises to the surface. Once boiling, reduce the heat to medium, partly cover with a lid and boil for 3 hours, stirring occasionally with a wooden spoon.

After 3 hours, reduce the heat to low and almost completely cover with the lid. Simmer for 1 hour. You should be able to crush the beans between your fingers. Strain through a fine-mesh sieve, discarding the remaining water. Leave the cooked soybeans in the sieve and let them cool down to approximately 25°C (77°F).

Line a metal tray with a clean tea towel (dish towel) and spread the soybeans out in an even layer. Scatter a handful of rice straw on top and cover with another tea towel. Place the tray inside the mini greenhouse set on top of the seedling heat mat and leave to ferment for around 36 hours.

Use two thermometers: one to ensure the greenhouse temperature stays around 26°C (79°F), and the other to monitor the soybean temperature, ensuring it stays around 30°C (86°F) and doesn't exceed 35°C (95°F).

After 36 hours, uncover the beans. Your cheonggukjang is well fermented if the beans have developed a layer of fine, white threads and have a sticky texture. Crush the beans to a paste using a pestle. Add the coarse sea salt and mix well. Divide the paste into portions and place in containers. Freeze for future use. For optimal flavour, use within 1 month.

GLUTINOUS RICE RED CHILLI PASTE
Chapsal gochujang 찹쌀고추장

MAKES 5 KG (11 LB)

Gochujang, along with doenjang, is a staple condiment made from red chilli, glutinous rice, fermented soybeans and salt. Its savoury, spicy and slightly sweet flavour profile makes it an essential ingredient for enhancing dishes like bibimbap (see page 137), or as a delicious accompaniment to lettuce wraps in Korean-style barbecue.

The process of making gochujang itself doesn't require a lengthy preparation; it can be completed within a day. However, the preparation of the fermented soybeans – one of the key ingredients in gochujang – can be time-consuming if you choose to use meju soybean blocks (see page 34). Alternatively, you can speed up the process by preparing the simplified soybean paste on page 40. Either way, it's worth noting that gochujang requires at least 1 year of aging, so planning ahead is essential.

500 g (1 lb 2 oz) glutinous rice flour
1.5 litres (51 fl oz/6 cups) Sikhye
  (page 244)
300 g (10½ oz) gochugaru
  (Korean red chilli powder)
200 g (7 oz) meju powder
  (soybean powder; see Tip)
200 g (7 oz) coarse sea salt
125 ml (4 fl oz/½ cup) Traditional
  Korean soup soy sauce
  (page 34)
60 ml (2 fl oz/¼ cup) soju
125 ml (4 fl oz/½ cup) Fermented
  fruit extract (page 20; made
  with the fruit of your choice)
sugar, for sprinkling

Add the glutinous rice flour to the sikhye in a saucepan. Mix well and bring to the boil over a medium heat. Continue stirring until the mixture forms a malt porridge and begins to thicken, then reduce the heat, cover with a lid and simmer for 10 minutes. Remove from the heat and leave to cool completely.

Combine the cooled porridge, gochugaru, meju powder, salt, soy sauce, soju and fruit extract in a large bowl and mix well.

Transfer to a fermenter and sprinkle a thick layer of sugar on the surface of the paste. The layer of sugar will harden over time, eventually forming a dry, crisp covering that will help prevent mould formation and minimise moisture loss.

You can begin using gochujang after a minimum of one year of aging. When using gochujang, carefully lift the layer of sugar. Scoop the gochujang with a dry spoon, then press down to fill the void. Cover it again with sugar. Cover the fermenter with a piece of muslin (cheesecloth) and store indefinitely in a well-ventialed, sheltered area with abundant sunlight.

TIP
Meju powder is made by grinding the meju blocks from the recipe on page 34. For a simplified method, you can use ground almeju (see page 40), or Sticky fermented soybean paste (page 47). Alternatively, meju powder is readily available at Korean and Asian grocers.

1

2

3

4

5

SALTED SEAFOOD
Jeotgal 젓갈

MAKES APPROX. 5 KG (11 LB)

Jeotgal, which translates to 'salted fermented seafood', is a staple condiment made by mixing various types of seafood with salt and allowing them to ferment over time. While anchovies and prawns (shrimp) are commonly used, in this recipe we are using sardines. Jeotgal is renowned for its robust and savoury flavour, and is frequently used to enhance dishes ranging from kimchi to various side dishes. The process of making jeotgal is relatively straightforward, but it is often prepared in larger batches and requires an extended preparation time. However, if this process seems daunting, store-bought jeotgal is readily available at Korean or Asian grocers.

Once you have made your jeotgal, an additional step can be taken to produce the byproduct, fish sauce, or aekjeot in Korean (see Tip). This versatile condiment is widely used to add an extra depth of flavour to various soups and side dishes.

5 kg (11 lb) whole sardines, rinsed in salted water
1 kg (2 lb 3 oz) coarse sea salt

Place the sardines in two to three large vacuum-seal bags. Divide the salt evenly between the bags. Seal and store in a cool, shaded area for at least 1 year.

After this time, jeotgal can be stored in a sealed glass jar for up to 1 year. Jeotgal is commonly blended into a paste before being added to seasonings to enhance their flavour.

TIP
Jeotgal aged for more than 2 years can be made into an aekjeot (fish sauce). Place the aged jeotgal in a large stockpot and bring to the boil over a high heat, then reduce the heat to medium and simmer for 20 minutes until the flesh breaks apart. Leave to cool, then filter through a fine-mesh sieve, collecting the fish sauce and discarding the solids. Store in a sealed glass jar at room temperature indefinitely.

1

2

3

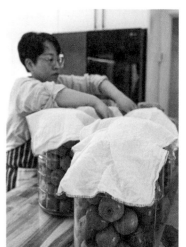

4

TRADITIONAL PERSIMMON VINEGAR
Gam sikcho 감식초

MAKES 5 LITRES (169 FL OZ)

This is the simplest way to prepare this traditional vinegar. Place the persimmons in a glass jar and allow nature to run its course. Over time, the fruit breaks down, producing a juice that gradually transforms into vinegar.

Thanks to its numerous health benefits and its unique blend of sour and sweet flavours, persimmon vinegar has become a staple condiment in dishes that require a touch of sourness. However, as with many other traditional Korean condiments, preparing persimmon vinegar can be a time-consuming process. It takes a minimum of 1 year for the persimmons to transform into vinegar, and the longer you age it the richer the flavour becomes. If you are short on time and space, store-bought persimmon vinegar can be used instead.

50 soft, ripe persimmons

Start by sterilising a 12 litre (405 fl oz) glass jar (see Tip, page 44), then dry completely. If any moisture remains in the jar, the vinegar will go off.

Wash the persimmons and dry them completely. Remove any imperfections on the fruit's surface with a knife. You do not have to remove the stem.

Place the persimmons in the sterile jar and thoroughly seal the top with plastic wrap. Pierce the wrap twice on top with a needle or fine skewer, then cover the plastic wrap with a cotton cloth to prevent fruit flies from entering the jar.

Leave the persimmon jar in a cool, dry place for 5–6 months. From about day 15 onwards, the persimmon juice will begin to gather at the bottom of the jar and a white film will gather on top.

After 5–6 months, separate the juice from the fruit by straining through a fine-mesh sieve. Discard the fruit and transfer the juice to a clean, sterilised jar (see Tip, page 44). Make it airtight by covering the mouth of the jar with a few layers of plastic wrap and securing it tightly with a rubber band. Leave to ferment for at least another 6 months.

After approximately 6 months, the fermented persimmon juice will naturally separate into two distinct layers. The upper layer will be clear, while the bottom will become cloudy due to sediment settling at the bottom. Carefully scoop out the clear upper part with a ladle and store in a sealed glass bottle in a cool dry place. The finished persimmon vinegar does not have an expiry date. (Discard the sediment from the bottom.)

Traditional persimmon vinegar (page 55)

여름

Yeoreum

SUMMER

SLICED RADISH KIMCHI
IN BRINE
62

WATERMELON RIND
KIMCHI
64

EGGPLANT KIMCHI
66

GREEN CABBAGE &
PERILLA LEAF
WHITE KIMCHI
69

STUFFED CUCUMBER
KIMCHI
72

COLD CUCUMBER &
SEAWEED SOUP
75

PICKLED CUCUMBER
76

PERILLA LEAF KIMCHI
79

PICKLED MELON
80

POTATO PANCAKES
WITH WATER CELERY
83

COLD SOYBEAN
MILK NOODLES
87

PERILLA OIL BUCKWHEAT
NOODLES
88

COLD EGGPLANT
SOUP
91

ACORN JELLY
IN BROTH
92

STEAMED BEEF
96

SEAFOOD SOYBEAN
PASTE SOUP
99

CHICKEN BREAST &
CUCUMBER SALAD
100

CINNAMON PUNCH
103

RED BEAN
SHAVED ICE
104

2023 Feb

KOREAN SUMMERS ARE HOT, SO WE EAT A LOT OF FRESH FOOD AND PRESERVES THAT WE'VE ALREADY MADE. NO ONE WANTS TO DO TOO MUCH COOKING WHEN IT'S HOT AND HUMID. NATURALLY, WE STILL MAKE KIMCHI BUT SUMMER KIMCHI IS BARELY OR LIGHTLY FERMENTED: IT'S ALL ABOUT FRESHNESS.

WHILE COLD DISHES LIKE COLD SOYBEAN MILK NOODLES OR CHICKEN BREAST AND CUCUMBER SALAD ARE WIDELY POPULAR, IT MIGHT SURPRISE YOU TO LEARN THAT KOREANS ALSO EAT A LOT OF HOT FOOD IN SUMMER. THERE IS A SAYING IN KOREAN, 'YI YUL CHI YUL', WHICH ROUGHLY TRANSLATES AS 'FIGHT FIRE WITH FIRE'. IN OTHER WORDS, YOU BEAT HEAT WITH HEAT. FOR EXAMPLE, WE EAT HOT, STEAMY CHICKEN SOUP WITH WARMING HERBS LIKE GINSENG AND JUJUBE. IT'S TO BALANCE THE ENERGY THAT YOU LOSE IN HOT WEATHER. OF COURSE, SUMMER VEGETABLES LIKE EGGPLANT (AUBERGINE), CUCUMBER AND ZUCCHINI (COURGETTE) ARE IMPORTANT IN THIS SEASON, TOO.

SLICED RADISH KIMCHI IN BRINE
Nabak-kimchi 나박김치

SERVES 10 AS A SIDE

This is the most well-known summer kimchi in my mum's hometown, Jeollanam-do, in the southern part of Korea. It's fresh, light and simple, using summer radish and pear, which make your body cooler. It's fermented for just 1 week.

Nabak-kimchi is a type of 'mul kimchi', which roughly translates as 'water kimchi'. Served in a bowl of cold stock, this dish is not only enjoyed as a side, but can also be quickly turned into a main meal with the addition of some noodles.

Nabak-kimchi is also part of the traditional dining table that we set for our ancestors around the New Year and Thanksgiving.

½ napa cabbage, outer leaves removed, inner leaves separated
½ daikon (white radish), cut into 3 cm (1¼ in) cubes
3 tablespoons coarse sea salt
3 tablespoons gochugaru (Korean red chilli powder)
150 g (5½ oz) mustard greens, cut into 3 cm (1¼ in) lengths
5 spring onions (scallions), cut into 3 cm (1¼ in) lengths
1 nashi pear, peeled, cut into eighths and deseeded
5 jujubes, deseeded
½ onion, thickly sliced

BROTH
250 g (9 oz/1 cup) Glutinous rice paste (page 21)
125 ml (4 fl oz/½ cup) Fermented fruit extract (page 20)
3 tablespoons coarse sea salt, or to taste

SPICE BAG
3 tablespoons minced garlic
1 tablespoon minced ginger

Cut the cabbage leaves into 3 × 3 cm (1¼ × 1¼ in) pieces and combine with the radish in a large (approximately 10 litre/338 fl oz) plastic storage container with a lid.

Add the salt and gochugaru and mix well, then leave to sit for 1 hour.

Prepare the broth by mixing 5 litres (169 fl oz) water with the glutinous rice paste, fruit extract and salt in a stockpot. Pour into the container with the cabbage and mix.

Make a spice bag by placing the minced garlic and ginger in a disposable tea bag (see Tip) to ensure your finished kimchi soup is clear. Put the tea bag in the container with the cabbage along with the mustard greens, spring onion, pear, jujubes and onion. Mix with a wooden spoon. Taste the soup at this point and, if it is too bland, add more salt. Add more water if the soup is too salty. (During fermentation the saltiness will subside a little, so, taking this into account, we suggest you season liberally prior to fermenting.)

Put the lid on the container and leave to sit at room temperature for 6 hours, then transfer to the fridge to continue fermenting. The radish kimchi will be ready after 1 week, and will keep in a sealed container for up to 3 months.

TIP
You can purchase packs of disposable, fillable tea bags online, and they come in handy for various infusions.

WATERMELON RIND KIMCHI
Soobak kimchi 수박김치

SERVES 4 AS A SIDE

My mum always made this for me in summer, but I have to admit I didn't love it when I was a child. Now I've come to appreciate the tangy flavour and crunchy texture. I also like that it's a creative way to reduce food waste and promote health, using up otherwise discarded watermelon and taking advantage of its high vitamin and fibre content.

You can eat this like a salad as soon as it's made – it isn't fermented at all – and finish the whole lot within a few days. Or add a spoonful of watermelon rind kimchi on top of your usual bibimbap (see page 137) ingredients to give everything a refreshing lift.

½ watermelon, rind removed
   and reserved
1 tablespoon coarse sea salt
1 teaspoon sesame oil
1 teaspoon sesame seeds

SEASONING
120 g (4½ oz/1 cup) chopped spring
   onion (scallion)
3 tablespoons gochugaru
   (Korean red chilli powder)
2 tablespoons Fermented fruit
   extract (page 20)
1 tablespoon salted shrimp
1 tablespoon minced garlic

Cut the watermelon rind into 3–4 cm (1¼–1½ in) thick slices, then julienne. Place in a bowl with the salt, mix well, then leave to sit for about 1 hour.

Rinse the rind under cold running water, then drain well.

Mix all the seasoning ingredients in a bowl with the rind. Cover and refrigerate until ready to serve.

Remove a portion of kimchi and add the sesame oil and sesame seeds right before serving.

As this kimchi is not fermented, I recommend consuming it within 3 days of making it.

1

2

3

EGGPLANT KIMCHI
Gaji kimchi 가지김치

SERVES 4 AS A SIDE

My family uses a lot of eggplant (aubergine) – steamed, fried and even fresh, like a carrot or radish as a sweet, crunchy snack. This nutritious, versatile side dish goes well with everything and my mum makes it all the time in summer – it's a very common dish in her town of Jeollanam-do. As is common with summer kimchi, this dish is lightly fermented and can be eaten on the same day it's made.

2 long, thin (Lebanese) eggplants
  (aubergines)
1 tablespoon coarse sea salt
½ teaspoon sesame seeds

SEASONING
50 g (1¾ oz/1 cup) snipped chives
1 red chilli, destemmed and
  chopped
3 tablespoons gochugaru
  (Korean red chilli powder)
2 tablespoons Fermented fruit
  extract (page 20)
1 tablespoon aekjeot (fish sauce)
1 tablespoon minced garlic

Trim the stem and blossom ends of the eggplants and cut crossways into 5 cm (2 in) rounds.

Combine the salt with 250 ml (8½ fl oz/1 cup) water in a bowl and add the eggplant. Leave to pickle for about 1 hour.

Once the eggplant is salted enough to bend easily, stand each piece on one cut end and score a deep cross down the middle, stopping 1 cm (½ in) from the base.

Mix all the seasoning ingredients together in a bowl. Take one piece of eggplant at a time and fill the slits with the seasoning.

Leave the eggplant to ferment at room temperature for approximately 2 hours, then garnish with sesame seeds before serving.

1

2

3

4

5

6

GREEN CABBAGE &
PERILLA LEAF WHITE KIMCHI

Yangbaechu kkaennip baek kimchi 양배추 깻잎 백김치

SERVES 4 AS A SIDE

This is a pretty, layered kimchi made with cabbage and perilla leaf, which gives it a unique fragrance. Fermented for a couple of days, it's often served with barbecue because the ingredients are very good for the stomach. We usually slice it to show off the colourful layers within each rolled cabbage parcel.

40 g (1½ oz) coarse sea salt
½ green cabbage, destemmed
150 g (5½ oz) mustard greens, roughly chopped
30 g (1 oz/½ cup) thinly sliced spring onion (scallion)
¼ onion, sliced
25 perilla leaves

SEASONING
125 g (4½ oz/½ cup) Glutinous rice paste (page 21)
60 g (2 oz) dried red chilli seeds (see Tip)
1½ tablespoons salted shrimp
1 tablespoon minced garlic
2 tablespoons Fermented fruit extract (page 20)

Combine the salt and 500 ml (17 fl oz/2 cups) water in a large bowl. Submerge the cabbage in the salted water, starting cut-side down and turning every hour, for about 5 hours, or until soft. Pick the cabbage leaves one by one.

Rinse the leaves under cold running water, then drain in a colander for an hour or two.

Combine all the seasoning ingredients in a bowl. Add the mustard greens, spring onion and onion, and mix well.

Rub the seasoning into the cabbage leaves, then place two or three perilla leaves on top of each seasoned cabbage leaf. Top with more seasoning, then repeat the layers until all the cabbage, perilla leaves and seasoning have been used.

Place in a container, seal and leave to ferment at room temperature for 12 hours, then transfer it to the refrigerator to continue fermenting for another 2 days.

Once fermented, the kimchi will keep in an airtight container in the fridge for 3–4 weeks.

TIP
You can buy dried red chilli seeds from nut shops, delis and Asian grocers.

Perilla leaf kimchi (page 79)

Stuffed cucumber kimchi (page 72)

STUFFED CUCUMBER KIMCHI
Oi sobagi 오이소박이

SERVES 4 AS A SIDE

We are always eating cucumbers in Korea, and especially in summer. They are about 97 per cent water, and so have a cooling effect on the body. You can think of this dish more as a salad than a preserve: make it and eat it within a week (and then make another batch!) because it's best when it's really crunchy and refreshing. Left for more than a week, it can become tangy and soggy. That's also why we don't add too much fish sauce or gochugaru: we want to highlight bright, fresh flavours.

5 Lebanese (short) cucumbers
1 tablespoon bicarbonate of soda (baking soda)
1 tablespoon coarse sea salt

STUFFING
15 g (½ oz) julienned carrots
20 g (¾ oz) chives, cut into 3 cm (1¼ in) lengths
½ red chilli, destemmed and sliced
¼ red onion, sliced

SEASONING
1 tablespoon gochugaru (Korean red chilli powder)
1 tablespoon Glutinous rice paste (page 21)
1 tablespoon salted shrimp
1 tablespoon Fermented fruit extract (page 20)
½ tablespoon aekjeot (fish sauce)
½ tablespoon minced garlic

Wash the cucumbers under cold running water and, using your hands, forcibly rub the skin with the bicarbonate of soda. Rinse well.

Combine the salt with 250 ml (8½ fl oz/1 cup) water in a bowl. Submerge the cucumbers in the salted water and leave to soak for 1 hour, or until they bend easily.

Once salted, briefly rinse the cucumbers under cold running water, then drain in a colander for about 1 hour.

Trim the stem and blossom ends of each cucumber, then cut in half crossways. Stand a cucumber half on its end and score a deep cross down the middle, stopping about 1 cm (½ in) from the base. Repeat with the remaining cucumbers.

Combine the stuffing and seasoning ingredients in a bowl and mix together well.

Tuck the stuffing inside the slits of the cucumber, then place in a container, cover and leave to ferment in the fridge for 1 day. After this, the cucumber kimchi will keep in the fridge for up to 1 week.

1

2

3

4

5

6

COLD CUCUMBER & SEAWEED SOUP

Oi miyeok naegguk 오이 미역 냉국

SERVES 4 AS A SIDE

We turn to this chilled miyeok (seaweed) soup on really hot days, either straight from the fridge or with the addition of ice cubes. The vinegar makes it even more refreshing. It's a very simple dish – the kind of boost you might need at lunchtime to spark you up for the afternoon.

5 g (⅛ oz) dried seaweed
2 Lebanese (short) cucumbers
1 tablespoon bicarbonate of soda (baking soda)
¼ onion, sliced
1 cayenne chilli, destemmed and julienned
1 teaspoon sesame seeds
ice cubes, to serve (optional)

BROTH
500 ml (17 fl oz/2 cups) cold water
1 tablespoon coarse sea salt
75 ml (2½ fl oz) Traditional persimmon vinegar (page 55), or apple-cider vinegar
60 ml (2 fl oz/¼ cup) Fermented fruit extract (page 20)

Soak the dried seaweed in cold water for about 10 minutes, then squeeze out the water with your hands. Cut into 2 cm (¾ in) pieces.

Wash the cucumbers under cold running water and, using your hands, forcibly rub the skin with the bicarbonate of soda. Rinse well.

Cut the cucumbers on the diagonal into 3–5 mm (⅛–¼ in) slices and finely julienne.

For the broth, combine all the ingredients in a bowl.

Add the cucumber, onion and chilli to the bowl of seasoning, followed by the sesame seeds. Cover and chill in the refrigerator for 2 hours.

If you'd like to enjoy it cooler, serve it with some ice cubes.

PICKLED CUCUMBER

Oiji 오이지

MAKES 15 AS A SIDE

'Oi' means cucumber and 'ji' means pickled so it's not hard to work out what this recipe is! We usually make this in big batches and keep it underground for ages, more or less forever. If you keep the cucumbers whole, they stay crunchy indefinitely. Not everyone can put their cucumber underground, of course, but oiji can still be preserved for years if they are sealed well, such as in a vacuum bag or a sterilised airtight glass jar (see Tip, page 44).

When we want to eat them, we remove some cucumbers and season them just before serving as banchan, a delightful small side dish.

Alongside kimchi, this is the most common thing Koreans have in the fridge. You will need to start this recipe 2 months before you plan to serve it.

15 Lebanese (short) cucumbers
3 tablespoons bicarbonate of soda
(baking soda)

BRINE
250 ml (8½ fl oz/1 cup) white
vinegar
250 ml (8½ fl oz/1 cup) Fermented
fruit extract (page 20)
125 ml (4 fl oz/½ cup) soju or sake
160 g (5½ oz/½ cup) coarse sea salt

SEASONING (FOR
5 CUCUMBERS)
1 tablespoon Fermented
fruit extract (page 20)
1 tablespoon gochugaru (Korean
red chilli powder)
¼ tablespoon minced garlic
½ tablespoon finely chopped
spring onion (scallion)
½ teaspoon sesame oil
sesame seeds, to serve

Wash the cucumbers under cold running water and, using your hands, forcibly rub the skin with the bicarbonate of soda. Rinse well, then leave to drain in a colander.

Combine the brine ingredients in a saucepan and bring to the boil over a high heat. When boiling, remove from the heat and leave to cool completely.

Ensure your cucumbers are thoroughly dry (pat dry with paper towel), then pack into a vacuum-sealed bag. Add the cooled brine, seal the bag and shake well. Leave to pickle for 1–2 months in the fridge.

Take five pickled cucumbers out of the bag and cut them into bite-sized pieces. Place in a bowl and mix with the fruit extract, then leave to sit for about 10 minutes to soak up the sweetness (the fruit extract helps to keep the cucumber crisp). After 10 minutes, add the remaining seasoning ingredients and mix well.

Stored in an airtight bag, these pickles will keep, unopened, for up to 1 year. Once opened, transfer the contents, including the brine, to a container with a secure lid. Store in the fridge for up to another year.

1

2

3

4

PERILLA LEAF KIMCHI
Kkaennip kimchi 깻잎 김치

SERVES 10 AS A SIDE

Perilla is ubiquitous: it grows like a weed in Korea, so we have lots of ways to use it. Open most Korean fridges and you'll find this kimchi. It's even available canned at grocers, ready to eat with everything – barbecue or with a bowl of rice. You can enjoy this banchan (small side dish) after aging it in the fridge for a day or so. Beyond that, it will keep in the fridge indefinitely.

50 perilla leaves
¼ onion, sliced
¼ carrot, peeled and julienned

SEASONING
80 ml (2½ fl oz/⅓ cup) All-purpose
    soy sauce (page 44)
2 tablespoons Fermented
    fruit extract (page 20)
2 tablespoons minced spring
    onion (scallion)
1 tablespoon cheongju
    (clear rice wine)
½ tablespoon gochugaru (Korean
    red chilli powder)
1 teaspoon minced red chilli
½ tablespoon minced garlic
1 teaspoon sesame oil
1 teaspoon sesame seeds

Wash the perilla leaves thoroughly under cold running water and drain in a colander.

Mix the seasoning ingredients together in a bowl. Add the onion and carrot and mix well.

Stack three or four perilla leaves and spread some seasoning on top. Repeat with the remaining perilla leaves and seasoning. Pack into an airtight container and ferment in the fridge for about 24 hours before serving. Store in the fridge for up to 1 year, removing your desired portion each time you would like to serve as banchan.

PICKLED MELON
Melon jangajji 멜론 장아찌

SERVES 16 AS A SIDE

The Chamoe melon, also known as Korean melon, has an oval shape and a smooth, thin, yellowish-green rind with faint white stripes. With its crisp texture and mild sweetness, Chamoe makes for an ideal and refreshing snack and it can even be pickled to create a delightful side dish that pairs well with various meals. However, this popular summer fruit is rare outside of Korea. To recreate this dish in Melbourne, I experimented with honeydew, using a similar technique to Pickled cucumber (page 76) and was very pleased with the results. At CHAE dining, I paired this pickled melon with tempura vegetables. Its refreshing, crisp, sweet and slightly sour profile complemented the dish, providing a delightful contrast to the overall richness. You will need to start this recipe 2 months before you plan to serve it.

2 honeydew melons

BRINE
125 ml (4 fl oz/½ cup) cheongju (clear rice wine)
250 ml (8½ fl oz/1 cup) white vinegar
250 ml (8½ fl oz/1 cup) Fermented fruit extract (page 20)
160 g (5½ oz/½ cup) coarse sea salt

SEASONING (FOR ¼ MELON)
2 tablespoons Fermented fruit extract (page 20)
1 teaspoon perilla oil (available at Asian grocers)
1 teaspoon sesame seeds

Combine the brine ingredients in a large bowl.

Trim the stem and blossom ends of the melons and remove the skin. Cut the flesh into eight wedges and remove the seeds.

Place the quartered melon in a vacuum-sealed bag.

Add the brine, seal the bag and shake well. Leave to pickle for 1–2 months in the fridge.

Take a quarter of pickled melon out of the bag and cut each wedge into bite-sized pieces. Place in a bowl and mix with the fruit extract, then leave to sit for about 10 minutes to soak up the sweetness (the extract helps to keep the melon crisp). After 10 minutes, add the perilla oil and sesame seeds to finish the pickle.

Stored in an airtight bag, these pickles will keep, unopened, for up to 1 year. Once opened, transfer the contents, including the brine, to a container with a secure lid. Store in the fridge for up to another year.

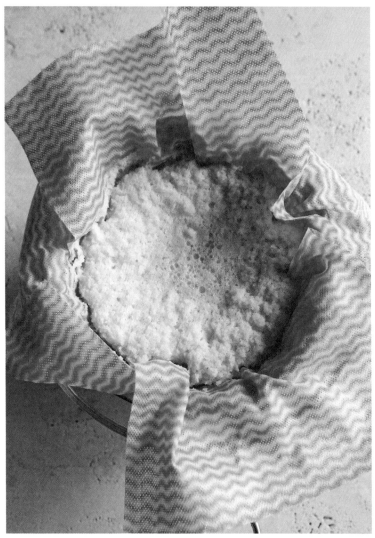

1

2

3

4

5

POTATO PANCAKES WITH WATER CELERY
Gamja-jeon & Minari cho-muchim 미나리 초무침 감자전

SERVES 2-3

Jeon (fritters or pancakes) are a bit of work to make so we tend to eat them for special family gatherings. The recipe technique involves grating the potatoes and squeezing the mixture to extract the starchy water. The starch is collected, then mixed back in with the potato. You end up with a crunchy shell and a chewy interior.

In this recipe we top the jeon with water celery, or minari in Korean. You can actually serve the fritters with any salad or pickle – in fact, the Pickled melon on page 80 would be a lovely accompaniment. They're delicious with makgeolli (cloudy rice wine), too.

3–4 whole russet (idaho) potatoes, peeled and cut into eighths
1 teaspoon salt
⅓ bunch of water celery (dropwort)
125 ml (4 fl oz/½ cup) vegetable oil
½ teaspoon sesame seeds, to garnish

WATER CELERY SEASONING
2 tablespoons Fermented fruit extract (page 20)
1 tablespoon All-purpose soy sauce (page 44)
1 tablespoon Traditional persimmon vinegar (page 55), or apple-cider vinegar
1 teaspoon sesame oil, plus extra to garnish
½ tablespoon gochugaru (Korean red chilli powder)
1 tablespoon minced spicy chilli (optional)

Finely purée the potato in a blender with 250 ml (8½ fl oz/1 cup) water.

Using a piece of muslin (cheesecloth) or a fine-mesh sieve, drain the potato and squeeze out and collect the juice in a bowl.

Set the potato juice aside for about 10 minutes so that the starch can settle. Remove the liquid on top with a spoon and collect the potato starch underneath. Mix the potato starch back in with the potato pulp and add the salt to make the potato pancake mix well.

While you're waiting for the potato starch to settle, make the water celery side dish.

Combine the water celery seasoning ingredients in a bowl, including the chilli, if using, and mix well. Wash the water celery under cold running water, then cut it into 5 cm (2 in) lengths, ready for blanching.

Bring a saucepan of salted water to the boil over a high heat and quickly blanch the water celery for 30 seconds. Immediately rinse the blanched water celery in cold water, then squeeze out the water by hand and place in a bowl.

Add the water celery seasoning to your liking.

Heat a frying pan over a medium heat and add the oil. Add the potato pancake mixture and use a spatula to spread it out into a disc about 7 cm (2¾ in) in diameter. Fry for 3 minutes, or until the underside is golden, then flip it over and cook until crisp and brown underneath, about another 3 minutes.

Place the fried potato pancake on a plate, top it with the seasoned water celery, and garnish with a drop of sesame oil and the sesame seeds.

Potato pancakes with water celery (page 83)

COLD SOYBEAN MILK NOODLES
Kong-guksu 콩국수

SERVES 2

Soybeans are endlessly useful. This chilled soymilk soup with noodles is a very popular dish, especially in summer. The soymilk can be seasoned with either salt or sugar, a choice that is distinctly personal, and often regional. For example, Yoora's family comes from Incheon and likes to add sugar for seasoning, while my family, originating in Jeolla-do, prefers salt.

This soymilk soup is versatile. Try blending it with your preferred fruits to create a nutritious and delicious smoothie, which makes a great addition to a busy morning routine. Use the soymilk soup within 2 days.

160 g (5½ oz) somyeon (thin wheat flour noodles)
½ tomato, sliced
½ cucumber, deseeded and thinly julienned
ice cubes, to serve

SOYMILK
200 g (7 oz/1 cup) dried soybeans
80 g (2¾ oz/½ cup) peanuts
2 tablespoons sesame seeds, plus extra to serve
½ tablespoon fine sea salt

Start by making the soymilk. Wash the soybeans thoroughly (at least twice) under cold running water. Soak the beans in lukewarm water for at least 6 hours.

Drain, and wash the soaked beans again under cold running water, then place them in a large saucepan and cover completely with water. Bring to the boil over a medium heat and cook for 20 minutes.

Drain the beans and rinse again under cold running water, then place in a blender with the peanuts, sesame seeds and 1 litre (34 fl oz/4 cups) water and blitz to a fine consistency.

Place your soymilk in the refrigerator to chill.

Bring a large pot of salted water to the boil, then add the noodles. (Stir with chopsticks to prevent the noodles from sticking together while boiling.) Once the water comes back to the boil, add 250 ml (8½ fl oz/1 cup) cold water and continue to stir the noodles over a high heat. When the water boils again, immediately drain the noodles and wash thoroughly under cold water as if you were washing your hair. This will remove the starch and ensure the noodles are chewy.

Divide the noodles neatly between serving bowls and pour over the soymilk. Add the tomato and cucumber on top, a few ice cubes and a sprinkling of sesame seeds before serving.

NOTES
Season with salt or sugar – whichever you prefer.

The soymilk doesn't have a very long shelf life. Store in the fridge and consume within 2 days.

PERILLA OIL BUCKWHEAT NOODLES

Deulgireum makguksu 들기름 막국수

SERVES 2

This is one of those 'nothing in the fridge' meals, relying on ready-made ingredients and just a few fresh items (which you can swap for other greens or even leave out). My mum would often make it for me in summer when the cupboards were a bit bare – it brings back really nice memories. Perilla oil is available from Asian grocers, but you could use sesame oil instead.

⅓ bunch of ssukgat
   (chrysanthemum greens;
   available at Asian grocers)
200 g (7 oz/2 cups) soybean
   sprouts
160 g (5½ oz) buckwheat noodles
5 g (¼ oz/½ cup) crushed roasted
   seaweed, to garnish
1 teaspoon ground sesame seeds,
   to garnish

VEGETABLE SEASONING
1 tablespoon Fermented fruit
   extract (page 20)
1 tablespoon All-purpose soy
   sauce (page 44)
½ tablespoon minced garlic
1 teaspoon sesame oil

NOODLE SEASONING
1 tablespoon Fermented fruit
   extract (page 20)
1 tablespoon All-purpose soy
   sauce (page 44)
1 tablespoon perilla oil

Prepare the vegetable seasoning by mixing all the ingredients together in a large bowl. Combine the noodle seasoning ingredients in another large bowl.

Wash the ssukgat under cold running water and trim into 3 cm (1¼ in) lengths. Wash the soybean sprouts and discard any heads that are brown, but keep the roots intact.

Bring a saucepan of water to the boil with a pinch of salt and blanch the greens and sprouts for approximately 30 seconds. Immediately drain and rinse under cold running water. Using your hands, squeeze out as much water as possible and mix with the prepared vegetable seasoning.

Bring another large saucepan of salted water to the boil and drop in the noodles. Stir with chopsticks to prevent them from clumping together. When the water starts to boil over, add 250 ml (8½ fl oz/ 1 cup) cold water and bring back to the boil, stirring with chopsticks. Once the water begins to boil again, pour the noodles into a colander. Rinse under cold running water as if you were washing your hair. This removes the starch, which will make the noodles chewy and firm.

Place the noodles in the bowl with the prepared noodle seasoning and mix to coat.

Place the seasoned noodles on a plate and place the seasoned chrysanthemum greens and soybean sprouts on top.

Garnish with the roasted seaweed and sesame seeds to elevate the flavours of this dish even further.

COLD EGGPLANT SOUP

Gaji naengguk 가지 냉국

SERVES 4 AS A SIDE

You might be starting to understand how much we love chilled soups in Korea! This cold eggplant (aubergine) soup is an easy starter that you eat immediately over ice. The eggplant can be pan-fried instead of steamed, if you prefer.

1 eggplant (aubergine), destemmed
1 tablespoon Traditional Korean soup soy sauce (page 34)
½ tablespoon minced garlic
1 tablespoon Traditional persimmon vinegar (page 55), or apple-cider vinegar
2 tablespoons Fermented fruit extract (page 20)
1 tablespoon chopped spring onion (scallion)
300 ml (10 fl oz) Anchovy & kelp broth (page 19)
ice cubes and sesame seeds, to serve

Wash the eggplant well under running water and cut it lengthways into four pieces.

Steam the eggplant using the double-boiler method. Set a colander over a saucepan of simmering water, making sure the water doesn't touch the base of the colander. Place the eggplant in the colander, cover with a lid and cook for about 5 minutes.

Remove the eggplant and leave to cool at room temperature. Tear the eggplant lengthways into pieces and place in a bowl.

Add the soy sauce, garlic, vinegar, fruit extract and spring onion to the eggplant and mix, then add the anchovy and kelp broth and mix with a wooden spoon. Season to taste with salt, then refrigerate until well chilled.

Serve with ice cubes and a sprinkling of sesame seeds.

ACORN JELLY IN BROTH

Dotori muk sabal 도토리 묵사발

SERVES 2

A lot of people don't realise that you can eat acorns, but it's normal for us. When we forage for them in Australia, people often ask why we have a bucket full of them. We explain that we take them home and dry them, then peel them and turn the nutty interior into a powder that can be hydrated and thickened into a jelly, similar to agar agar. It's a long process though, so you might be glad to know that acorn powder (which can be hydrated to form a jelly) is also available at Korean grocers.

We would have this dish every summer, either hot or cold. The jelly can also be a simple side dish, seasoned with soy sauce. When checking the jelly, look for a texture that's firm but still floppy.

300 g (10½ oz) Acorn jelly
    (see below)
½ teaspoon vegetable oil
1 egg, beaten
185 g (6½ oz/1 cup) cooked
    medium-grain rice
1 litre (34 fl oz/4 cups) Anchovy
    & kelp broth (page 19)
½ cayenne chilli, destemmed
    and finely chopped
1 teaspoon chopped spring onion
    (scallion)
1 tablespoon crushed roasted
    seaweed
sesame seeds, to serve

ACORN JELLY
50 g (1¾ oz) acorn powder
    (available at Korean or Asian
    grocers)
250 ml (8½ fl oz/1 cup) lukewarm
    water
1 teaspoon sesame oil
½ teaspoon fine sea salt

KIMCHI TOPPING
200 g (7 oz/1 cup) well-fermented
    ripe Cabbage kimchi (page 158)
1 teaspoon sesame oil
1 tablespoon Fermented fruit
    extract (page 20)
½ teaspoon sesame seeds

Start by making the acorn jelly. Mix the acorn powder into the lukewarm water in a saucepan and bring to the boil over a medium heat. Once the mixture starts to boil, lower the heat and stir frequently with a spatula so it doesn't stick and burn on the bottom of the pan. When small bubbles start to form on the surface, add the sesame oil and a pinch of salt. Stir for another 5 minutes, until the mixture is thick when scooped with the spatula, then turn off the heat. Cover with a lid and rest for about 10 minutes.

Transfer the mixture to a container and flatten the top. Leave the jelly to cool completely.

Place a frying pan over a low heat and rub a thin layer of vegetable oil over the surface using a paper towel. Add the beaten egg and cook slowly into a small omelette for 2–3 minutes, then flip over and cook on the other side for a further minute, ensuring that the egg doesn't brown. Once cooked, cut the omelette into very thin strips.

For the kimchi topping, squeeze out as much juice as possible with your hands, chop the kimchi on a wooden board, then add the sesame oil, fruit extract and sesame seeds and mix well.

Combine all the soy sauce seasoning ingredients in a bowl.

Cut the cold acorn jelly into 3 × 3 cm (1¼ × 1¼ in) pieces about 1 cm (½ in) thick. Warm the anchovy and kelp broth.

To serve, divide the rice between two bowls and top each with half the acorn jelly. Garnish with kimchi and egg strips, then pour the warm anchovy broth over the top and finish with the chilli, spring onion, crushed seaweed and sesame seeds. Add soy sauce seasoning to taste.

SOY SAUCE SEASONING

2 tablespoons All-purpose soy
    sauce (page 44)
1 tablespoon chopped spring
    onion (scallion)
1 teaspoon gochugaru (Korean
    red chilli powder)
1 teaspoon sesame oil
1 teaspoon minced garlic
1 teaspoon ground sesame seeds

1

2

3

5

4

Acorn jelly in broth (page 92)

STEAMED BEEF

Sogogi-jjim 소고기찜

SERVES 2

Rolled and steamed, this is a very simple beef dish with gentle core flavours and a bright seasoning to tie it together. It's quite casual in style and is often served on a shared platter. There's a very personal reason why I don't serve it share-style though. My mum was born shortly after the Korean War when beef was very scarce and considered a luxurious ingredient. Throughout my childhood, I very rarely saw my mum eat any meat – she would wait until I had finished. Even now, my mum feels guilty eating beef, but I know that she does love the flavour and texture. So, when I make this for her, I give her an individual portion. It's my way of signalling to her that it's okay, you have your own beef, eat it and enjoy it. And she does!

4 napa cabbage leaves
150 g (5½ oz) scotch fillet
    (ribeye steak), cut into
    2 mm (⅛ in) slices
100 g (3½ oz) enoki mushrooms
5 g (⅛ oz) chopped red and green
    chilli, to garnish

SEASONING DIPPING
SAUCE
2 tablespoons All-purpose soy
    sauce (page 44)
2 tablespoons Fermented fruit
    extract (page 20)
1 tablespoon Traditional
    persimmon vinegar (page 55),
    or apple-cider vinegar
1 teaspoon sesame oil
1 teaspoon crushed sesame seeds
1 teaspoon wasabi paste

Bring a saucepan of water to the boil with a pinch of salt. Briefly blanch the cabbage leaves in the water for about 30 seconds, then immediately drain and rinse under cold running water. Using your hands, gently squeeze out as much water as possible.

Top each of the cabbage leaves with equal amounts of sliced beef and enoki mushrooms, then roll up tightly.

Set a steamer over a saucepan of boiling water and boil over a high heat for about 10 minutes.

In the meantime, prepare the dipping sauce by combining all the ingredients in a bowl. Mix well.

To serve, garnish the steamed cabbage rolls with the chopped chilli and drizzle with the dipping sauce, or serve on the side.

SEAFOOD SOYBEAN PASTE SOUP

Haemul doenjang jjigae 해물 된장찌개

SERVES 3

Jjigae is a Korean soup or stew, and this version is one of the most popular, enjoyed all year round. It's endlessly adaptable. My grandma loved to use mussels, but any seafood is fine. You could even do the same dish with beef, or leave meat out altogether and do it with tofu and vegetables in kelp stock.

The key to this dish is the doenjang (soybean paste), which is so much better when it's home-made (see page 34).

1 tablespoon Traditional Korean soybean paste (page 34)
½ tablespoon gochugaru (Korean red chilli powder)
1.5 litres (51 fl oz/6 cups) Anchovy & kelp broth (page 19)
250 g (9 oz) seafood marinara
150 g (5½ oz) firm tofu
½ onion, diced
½ zucchini (courgette), diced
1 spring onion (scallion), trimmed and sliced diagonally
1 red bullet chilli, destemmed and sliced diagonally

Add the soybean paste and gochugaru to the anchovy and kelp broth, mix well and bring to the boil over a medium heat.

Add the seafood and allow the broth to come back to the boil, then reduce the heat to low and simmer for another 10 minutes.

Add the tofu, onion and zucchini to simmer for another 5 minutes.

Add the spring onion and chilli and continue simmer for another couple of minutes before serving.

CHICKEN BREAST & CUCUMBER SALAD

Dak-gaseumsal oi-naengchae 닭가슴살 오이 냉채

SERVES 2

Summer salads are typically served with a mustard dressing: it's perfect for hot weather. The classic naengchae (salad) is with jellyfish but I do chicken instead. Because I still want the jellyfish texture, I also add konjac noodles, which have a jelly-like bite to them. This is a lovely dish to put in the centre of the table to share, but you can also serve it individually in small portions as part of a multi-course banquet.

2 tablespoons cheongju
    (clear rice wine)
1 tablespoon lemon juice
1 pinch coarse sea salt
180 g (6½ oz) chicken breast
¼ onion, thinly sliced
50 g (1¾ oz) bean sprouts
100 g (3½ oz) konjac noodles,
    washed and drained
1 Lebanese (short) cucumber,
    deseeded and julienned
2 capsicums (bell peppers),
    1 green and 1 red, thinly sliced
1 spring onion (scallion), thinly
    sliced diagonally, to garnish
½ teaspoon ground sesame seeds,
    to garnish

SAUCE SEASONING

3 tablespoons Traditional
    persimmon vinegar (page 55),
    or apple-cider vinegar
2 tablespoons All-purpose soy
    sauce (page 44)
2 tablespoons Fermented fruit
    extract (page 20)
½ tablespoon dijon mustard
½ tablespoon wholegrain mustard
½ tablespoon minced garlic
1 teaspoon sesame oil

CHICKEN SEASONING

1 tablespoon Fermented fruit
    extract (page 20)
1 teaspoon cheongju (clear rice
    wine) or soju
1 pinch of fine sea salt
1 pinch of cracked black pepper

Bring 750 ml (25½ fl oz/3 cups) water to the boil in a large saucepan and add the cheongju, lemon juice and salt. Add the chicken breast, reduce the heat to low and simmer for 10–15 minutes. Remove and leave to cool.

Soak the onion in water for 10 minutes to soften the flavour, then drain in a sieve.

Bring another saucepan of salted water to the boil and blanch the bean sprouts for about 20 seconds. Immediately plunge into cold water, then drain and squeeze the water out with your hands.

Shred the cooled chicken breast into strips.

Combine the sauce seasoning ingredients in a bowl and mix well.

Combine the chicken seasoning ingredients in another small bowl.

Combine the chicken, konjac noodles and all the vegetables in a bowl and season with the chicken seasoning. Place it neatly in the middle of a serving plate.

Place the cucumber and capsicum neatly in a row on top of the chicken and konjac. Sprinkle the sauce on top and garnish with spring onion and sesame seeds.

CINNAMON PUNCH

Sujeonggwa 수정과

SERVES 4

Sujeonggwa is a traditional Korean beverage with a rich cultural heritage. I would always be given sujeonggwa at Grandma's house but I didn't really appreciate the zesty cinnamon bite until I was older. The spice notes make it a very good dessert drink after a heavy meal. You can be flexible with the sweetener: maple syrup or agave syrup are good substitutes for the jocheong (rice syrup).

7–8 short cinnamon sticks
15 g (½ oz) piece ginger, peeled, washed and sliced
75 g (2¾ oz) jocheong (rice syrup), or agave or maple syrup

GARNISH (PER SERVE)
1 teaspoon pine nuts, crushed
1 teaspoon walnuts, crushed
1–2 jujubes, deseeded

Fill two saucepans with 750 ml (25 fl oz/3 cups) water each and bring to a simmer over a medium heat. Add the cinnamon sticks to one and the sliced ginger to the other and simmer for 30 minutes.

Combine the two infused waters in a clean saucepan by draining them through a fine-mesh sieve. Discard the cinnamon sticks and ginger. Add the jocheong and bring to the boil.

After 10 minutes, remove the punch from the heat, pour it into a container and chill in the fridge.

You can serve sujeonggwa cold, or heat it and enjoy it like tea.

Garnish with the crushed pine nuts and walnuts. Flatten the jujubes, roll and slice them horizontally into a flower shape and add these as well.

RED BEAN SHAVED ICE
Pat-bingsu 팥빙수

SERVES 4

This is a very well-known street food snack and dessert that comes in so many different versions and is especially popular in summer. Kids – and kids at heart – all love it. It's something people usually go out for, rather than making at home, and you do need a shaved ice machine to make it properly. The garnishes here – red bean paste, milk jam, rice balls and soybean powder – are very traditional. A more contemporary approach using fruit toppings is equally popular.

500 ml (17 fl oz/2 cups) full-cream (whole) milk, or milk of your choice
1 tablespoon dried soybeans

RED BEAN PASTE
100 g (3½ oz) dried adzuki beans
50 ml (1¾ fl oz) Fermented fruit extract (page 20)
1 tablespoon jocheong (rice syrup)
pinch of sea salt

GYEONGDAN (RICE BALLS)
50 g (1¾ oz) glutinous rice flour
pinch of sea salt
1 teaspoon Fermented fruit extract (page 20)
½ tablespoon hot water
1 tablespoon jocheong (rice syrup)

MILK JAM
150 ml (5 fl oz) full-cream (whole) milk, or milk of your choice
2 tablespoons jocheong (rice syrup)

Start this recipe the day before. Freeze the milk in a container.

ADZUKI BEANS
You don't need to soak the adzuki beans in advance. Wash the beans thoroughly twice, then place them in a saucepan and cover with water.

Bring to the boil over a high heat and, once boiling, drain the beans. Return the beans to the saucepan and cover with four or five times the amount of cold water. Again, bring the beans to the boil over a medium heat, then reduce the heat to low and simmer for about 1 hour.

Add the fruit extract, jocheong and sea salt. Cook for another 20–30 minutes, or until the beans have softened and you can easily crush one between your fingers (check regularly to avoid overcooking). Remove from the heat and leave to cool.

RICE BALLS
In the meantime, make the rice balls. Mix the glutinous rice flour with the salt, then add the fruit extract. Slowly add the hot water, being careful to add only enough so the dough doesn't stick, then knead well. (The dough can be very hot, so it's a good idea to mix with a wooden spoon initially to avoid burning your hands.)

Divide the dough into 15 g (½ oz) pieces and roll into balls. Set aside.

MILK JAM
Combine the milk and jocheong in a saucepan and bring to the boil over a medium heat. Reduce the heat to low and cook for about 1 hour until the milk just begins to caramelise, then turn off the heat.

Filter the milk jam through a fine-mesh sieve and leave to cool completely.

To bring the dish together, wash the soybeans, then place them in a dry frying pan set over a low heat and roast until golden, about 10 minutes.

Finely grind the roasted beans in a spice grinder.

Bring a saucepan of salted water to the boil and add the rice balls.

When the rice balls float to the surface, they are cooked. Remove and wash them under cold running water, then mix them with the jocheong.

Finely shave the frozen milk with an ice shaver and scoop it into serving bowls. Top each with a generous amount of red bean paste.

Top this with the syrup-covered rice balls (see Tip) and drizzle over the milk jam.

Add the roasted soybean powder on top and serve.

TIP
Preparing the rice balls immediately before serving them is more delicious.

가을

Ga-eul

AUTUMN

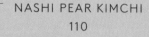

NASHI PEAR KIMCHI
110

WHITE DICED
RADISH KIMCHI
112

TRADITIONAL
RADISH KIMCHI
114

FRESH NAPA KIMCHI
115

POMEGRANATE KIMCHI
116

FRIED EGGPLANT
120

SEASONED DRIED
RADISH STRIPS
122

DRIED RADISH GREENS
IN SOYBEAN PASTE
123

STEAMED NAPA CABBAGE
WITH CHILLI OIL
126

MONKFISH FISH
BALL SOUP
129

STIR-FRIED BEEF
GOCHUJANG
130

BRAISED MACKEREL
133

PORK KIMCHI STEW
134

CHESTNUT RICE
STONE BOWL WITH
SEASONAL HERBS
137

RICE CAKE WITH
BEEF SPARE RIB SOUP
143

PEAR GINGER TEA
144

ORANGE EXTRACT
SHAVED ICE
148

TRADITIONAL KOREAN
RICE DOUGHNUT
151

SUMMER IS LONG AND AUTUMN COMES ON QUICKLY IN
KOREA: WE HARVEST AND THEN WE START TO PRESERVE.
AUTUMN IS A VERY DRY SEASON SO WE TAKE ADVANTAGE OF
THE CONDITIONS TO DO A LOT OF DRYING AND DEHYDRATING.
IN KOREA, WE CAN DO ALL THIS OUTSIDE, BUT WHERE WE
ARE IN AUSTRALIA WE USUALLY NEED TO HANG INGREDIENTS
INSIDE OR USE A DEHYDRATOR TO GET THE SAME RESULT.
WE DRY ALL KINDS OF THINGS: VEGETABLES, CHESTNUTS AND
EVEN ACORNS. WE HAVE A LOT OF FESTIVALS AT THIS TIME
OF YEAR, TOO, INCLUDING CHUSEOK, OR THANKSGIVING.
IT'S ALSO A TIME OF ABUNDANT PEARS AND LATE-SUMMER
VEGETABLES LIKE EGGPLANT (AUBERGINE) AND RADISHES.

NASHI PEAR KIMCHI
Bae kkakdugi 배깍두기

SERVES 2 AS A SIDE

This kimchi is like a salad, eaten immediately with no fermentation, and preferably finished on the day it's made, and certainly within 3 days. The longer you leave it, the more watery and soggy it becomes. We like this with steamed beef or pork.

3 nashi pears, peeled
25 g (1 oz/½ cup) garlic chives,
  washed and snipped
  into 2 cm (¾ in) lengths
sesame seeds, to taste

SEASONING
1 tablespoon gochugaru
  (Korean red chilli powder)
1 tablespoon minced garlic
1 tablespoon Fermented fruit
  extract (page 20)
1 tablespoon aekjeot (fish sauce)
½ tablespoon salted shrimp

Prepare the seasoning by combining all the ingredients in a bowl.

Cut the pear into quarters and remove the seeds. Again, cut each piece of quartered pear lengthways into quarters and place in a bowl.

Add the snipped chives to the bowl with the pears.

Add the prepared seasoning and mix well, then sprinkle with the sesame seeds before serving.

WHITE DICED RADISH KIMCHI
Baek kkakdugi 백깍두기

SERVES 10 AS A SIDE

This is similar to the Nashi pear kimchi (page 110), but it's fermented for a week and it doesn't include chilli. 'Baek' means white, denoting the absence of the gochugaru (Korean red chilli powder) that would turn the dish red. Because of the lack of heat, it's a popular kimchi for children. You can enjoy it with just about anything. It's great with pork belly or other greasy foods because it's very fresh and tart.

Any sweet red apple will work well and you could also use pear if that's what you have in the fruit bowl.

2 daikon (white radishes), destemmed
2 tablespoons coarse sea salt
2 sweet red apples
25 g (1 oz/½ cup) garlic chives, cut into 2 cm (¾ in) lengths

SEASONING
150 g (5½ oz/½ cup) Glutinous rice paste (page 21)
3 tablespoons aekjeot (fish sauce)
3 tablespoons Fermented fruit extract (page 20)
2 tablespoons minced garlic
1 tablespoon salted shrimp
1 teaspoon minced ginger

Peel and cut the daikon into 2 cm (¾ in) cubes and place in a bowl. Sprinkle the salt over the radish and leave for approximately 1 hour.

Wash the salted radish quickly under cold running water and drain in a sieve.

Peel and core the apples and cut the flesh into bite-sized cubes, like the radish.

Mix the prepared seasoning ingredients in a bowl.

Mix the radish, apple and chives with the seasoning in a container, seal and leave to ferment at room temperature for 24 hours.

Transfer it to the fridge and ferment for another week before eating. This kimchi will keep for up to 3 weeks stored in a sealed container.

TRADITIONAL RADISH KIMCHI
Seokbakji 석박지

SERVES 10 AS A SIDE

Seokbakji is chopped in random rough chunks as distinct from Kkakdugi (page 212), which is cut into perfect squares.

This is a simple, quick recipe and you might be surprised to see Sprite as an ingredient, but the soft drink is actually a widely used fermentation shortcut in Korea. It speeds up the process because of the sugar content.

This kimchi is properly ready when it's fermented for roughly 2 weeks, but it also tastes excellent along the way. After a week, you can start eating it with substantial bone broth soups, such as Rice cake with beef spare rib soup (page 143). As the radish ferments, it releases a lot of kimchi juice, which can be used as a base for cold, tangy noodle soups. Once it's ready, this kimchi is great with pork belly or anything rich and fatty.

2 daikon (white radishes), destemmed
2 tablespoons coarse sea salt

SEASONING
250 ml (8½ fl oz/1 cup) Sprite, or other lemonade
125 g (4½ oz/½ cup) Glutinous rice paste (page 21)
50 g (1¾ oz) gochugaru (Korean red chilli powder)
3 tablespoons aekjeot (fish sauce)
3 tablespoons Fermented fruit extract (page 20)
2 tablespoons minced garlic
1 tablespoon salted shrimp

Peel the daikon and cut into relatively thick chunks that would still be comfortable to eat, then place in a bowl. Sprinkle the salt over the radish and leave for approximately 1 hour.

Wash the salted radish quickly under cold running water and drain in a sieve.

Mix the seasoning ingredients together in a bowl.

Mix the radish with the seasoning in a container, seal and leave to ferment at room temperature for 24 hours. Transfer it to the fridge and ferment for another week before eating.

Kimchi can be stored indefinitely in the fridge provided the vegetables are submerged in the brine so they don't dry out and become mouldy. Store in a sealed container.

FRESH NAPA KIMCHI
Gutjuri 겉절이

SERVES 10 AS A SIDE

This kimchi, widely enjoyed with bossam (pork wraps, page 195), should be prepared on the day you're going to eat it. The cabbage is heavily salted for an hour to soften it, but the seasoning is quite sweet to balance it out. It works so well with pork.

My mum holds the cabbage in the air and cuts it on the diagonal to get the distinct gutjuri shape, but maybe it's safer if you use a chopping board!

315 g (11 oz/1 cup) coarse sea salt
½ napa cabbage
¼ daikon (white radish), destemmed, peeled and thinly julienned
70 g (2½ oz) spring onions (scallions), trimmed and cut into 4 cm (1½ in) lengths
1 teaspoon sesame seeds

SEASONING
3 tablespoons Fermented fruit extract (page 20)
1 tablespoon minced garlic
3 tablespoons aekjeot (fish sauce)
1 tablespoon salted shrimp
1 teaspoon minced ginger
100 g (3½ oz) gochugaru (Korean red chilli powder)

Combine the salt with 1.25 litres (42 fl oz/5 cups) water in a bowl to make a brine.

Halve the cabbage and cut around the firm stem to remove it, then halve the cabbage pieces again lengthways, then slice diagonally. You can leave the smaller central leaves whole.

Soak the cabbage in the brine for about an hour, turning it every 20 minutes.

Once the cabbage leaves have softened enough to bend easily, drain, then rinse under cold running water three or four times. Leave the cabbage to drain in a colander.

Combine all the seasoning ingredients, except the gochugaru, in a blender and blitz.

Place the seasoning in a bowl and mix in the gochugaru. Add the cabbage, daikon and spring onion, mix well, then serve immediately scattered with sesame seeds.

POMEGRANATE KIMCHI

Sukryu kimchi 석류김치

SERVES 10 AS A SIDE

When you have very important guests coming over, you might prepare this elaborate kimchi, which requires many ingredients, quite a lot of time, and fine knife work. Radishes are finely scored, stuffed, then wrapped in cabbage leaves to ferment. Despite the name, there's no pomegranate in this recipe – the name refers to the appearance, which recalls a split pomegranate with its arils exposed.

Raw chestnuts can be a tricky ingredient. To assist in peeling, you can cut a little cross in the shell and warm them in a microwave to loosen the skin.

2 daikon (white radishes), destemmed
30 g (1 oz) coarse sea salt
10 large napa cabbage leaves
5 dried black fungus (wood ears)
125 ml (4 fl oz/½ cup) Anchovy & kelp broth (page 19)

KIMCHI FILLING
6 jujubes, deseeded
¼ daikon (white radish), destemmed, peeled and julienned
6 chestnuts, shells removed, julienned
55 g (2 oz/1 cup) mustard greens, cut into 3 cm (1¼ in) lengths
45 g (1½ oz/1 cup) chives, cut into 3 cm (1¼ in) lengths
1 cayenne chilli, destemmed and finely sliced
1 green chilli, destemmed, deseeded and julienned

KIMCHI SEASONING
250 g (9 oz/1 cup) Glutinous rice paste (page 21)
80 ml (2½ fl oz/⅓ cup) aekjeot (fish sauce)
2 tablespoons minced garlic
3 cm (1¼ in) piece of ginger, peeled and julienned

Peel and cut the daikon crossways into 6 cm (2½ in) slices. Place the slices on one cut side and deeply score the other cut side in a crosshatch pattern, leaving the bottom 1 cm (½ in) uncut so the radish doesn't break apart.

Combine the salt with 1 litre (34 fl oz/4 cups) water in a container. Add the radish, crosshatched surfaces facing downwards, then add the cabbage leaves and leave for 2 hours.

Soak the dried black fungus in a bowl of lukewarm water for 1 hour, then rinse and julienne finely.

Next, prepare the kimchi filling. Run your knife along the flesh side of each half jujube to flatten it out. Julienne, then combine with the rest of the filling ingredients in a bowl.

Mix all the kimchi seasoning ingredients in a bowl, then mix thoroughly with the prepared filling.

Drain the radish and cabbage and carefully stuff the crosshatches in the radish with the filling.

Wrap each piece of radish in a napa cabbage leaf and place, side by side, in a container. Mix the left-over filling with the anchovy and kelp broth and pour into the container, seal and leave to ferment at room temperature for 24 hours, then refrigerate in a sealed container and consume within a week.

1

2

3

Pomegranate kimchi (page 116)

FRIED EGGPLANT
Gaji twigim 가지튀김

SERVES 3

Eggplant (aubergine) is plentiful at the end of summer as it turns to autumn, so we find lots of ways to eat it. Typically, it's steamed and mixed with soy, vinegar, chilli and garlic, but it's an acquired taste. In fact, Yoora doesn't like eggplant at all – except for this fried version. Maybe you'll also find that this is an eggplant dish that seduces eggplant haters! Battered, fried and served with a spicy dipping sauce, these eggplant pieces are crunchy on the outside and soft and juicy on the inside. I love to snack on them as soon as they're cooked.

1 eggplant (aubergine),
    destemmed
iced water, for the batter
2 litres (68 fl oz/8 cups) vegetable
    oil, for deep-frying

DRY BATTER
150 g (5½ oz/1 cup) plain
    (all-purpose) flour
3 tablespoons cornflour
    (cornstarch)
2 teaspoons garlic powder
1 teaspoon onion powder
1 teaspoon baking powder

DIPPING SAUCE
1 tablespoon All-purpose soy
    sauce (page 44)
1 tablespoon Traditional
    persimmon vinegar (page 55),
    or apple-cider vinegar
½ tablespoon gochugaru (Korean
    red chilli powder)

Cut the eggplant into bite-sized pieces. Place in a bowl and season with salt.

Mix all the batter ingredients together in a large bowl, add the eggplant and toss to coat. Remove the dusted eggplant from the batter and set aside.

To the remaining dry batter mix, add one-and-a-half times the quantity of iced water and mix well.

Heat the oil in a deep-fryer or large pot to 170–180°C (338–356°F). If you do not have a cooking thermometer, pick up some batter with chopsticks and drop it in the oil. If it sinks halfway down, then immediately rises to the top, the oil is ready.

Working in small batches, dip the dusted eggplant in the batter, turning to coat, then fry in the hot oil. Don't overcrowd the pot, as this will drop the oil temperature, causing your batter to become soggy. Once the eggplant rises to the surface, use chopsticks to flip it over until all sides are golden brown and crisp. Remove from the oil and place on a wire rack to cool.

Mix all the ingredients together for the dipping sauce and serve it with the crispy eggplant fries.

SEASONED DRIED RADISH STRIPS
Mumallaengi muchim 무말랭이 무침

SERVES 10 AS A SIDE

Collecting seasonal produce and drying it at its peak is the best way to preserve key nutritional ingredients for future use.

In my younger days, I vividly recall observing families and neighbours diligently laying out strips of radish to sun-dry them – a tradition that has somewhat waned in recent times. Nowadays, readily available, store-bought bags of dried radish have replaced this practice, and for those equipped with a dehydrator, the process can be conveniently replicated at home.

This recipe is a very simple way to use dried radish: soaked in warm water, then marinated to create a crunchy side dish. Often paired with fresh Cabbage kimchi (page 158), this preparation stands as a beloved accompaniment to bossam (pork wraps, page 195), though its versatility extends to virtually any meal. For an extra dimension of flavour, consider adding fermented chilli leaves or chilli to taste.

100 g (3½ oz) dried radish
(see Note)
1 litre (34 fl oz/4 cups) lukewarm
water
2 tablespoons jocheong (rice
syrup), or Fermented fruit
extract (page 20)

SEASONING
2 tablespoons gochugaru
(Korean red chilli powder)
3 tablespoons All-purpose soy
sauce (page 44), plus extra
if needed
1 tablespoon minced garlic
1 tablespoon sesame oil
2 tablespoons Fermented fruit
extract (page 20)
60 g (2 oz/½ cup) chopped spring
onion (scallion)
sesame seeds, to serve

Wash the dried radish under cold running water, then place in a bowl with the lukewarm water and jocheong or fermented fruit extract and soak for about 30 minutes.

Combine all the seasoning ingredients, except the spring onion and sesame seeds, in a bowl and mix well.

Thoroughly rinse the radish until the water becomes clear. Squeeze the rinsed radish to remove any excess water and place it in a bowl.

Add the seasoning mix and spring onion to the radish and taste. If it lacks flavour, add some more all-purpose soy sauce to taste. Sprinkle with the sesame seeds before serving.

DRIED RADISH GREENS IN SOYBEAN PASTE

Doenjang mucheong-siraegi 무청시래기 된장지짐

SERVES 4 AS A SIDE

This is one of my favourite dishes, a hometown vegetable recipe of my mum's that she would make for me. It gives me cosy memories. During autumn when radishes are plentiful, we use the radish root and also the leaves. We boil, then dry the leaves to make siraegi, which we keep for the whole year. When I use them, it reminds me of my mum's outside work area, with radish greens, garlic and onions all strung out to dry.

To make this dish, the dried radish greens are soaked and boiled again, cooked with seasonings, then eaten with rice. It's important to use a very good soybean paste, well aged with lots of umami flavour.

50 g (1¾ oz) dried radish greens (available at Asian grocers)
250 ml (8½ fl oz/1 cup) Anchovy & kelp broth (page 19)
2 tablespoons perilla powder (available at Asian grocers)
1 teaspoon sesame seeds

SEASONING
1 tablespoon minced garlic
1 tablespoon Fermented fruit extract (page 20)
1 tablespoon perilla oil (available at Asian grocers)
1 tablespoon chopped spring onion (scallion)
1 tablespoon Traditional Korean soybean paste (page 34)
1 teaspoon Traditional Korean soup soy sauce (page 34)

Soak the dried radish greens in a bowl of warm water for about 6 hours.

Thoroughly wash the soaked radish greens several times to remove any foreign substances and soil, then place in a saucepan and cover with plenty of water. Bring to the boil over a medium heat, then simmer for about 1 hour until soft.

Once cooked, drain and wash the radish greens under cold running water, then squeeze out any excess with your hands. Peel off the outer layer of the radish greens. (If the skin doesn't peel away easily, it hasn't been boiled for long enough. Return to the saucepan, cover with water and boil for another 10–15 minutes, if needed.)

Cut the radish greens into 5 cm (2 in) lengths and combine with the seasoning ingredients in a bowl, rubbing the seasoning well into the radish greens.

Place a dry frying pan over a medium heat and stir-fry the seasoned radish greens for about 1 minute, then add the anchovy and kelp broth and the perilla powder and simmer for 10 minutes, or until the liquid reduces by almost half.

Remove from the heat and sprinkle the sesame seeds on top. Serve with rice.

Dried radish greens in soybean paste (page 123)

STEAMED NAPA CABBAGE
WITH CHILLI OIL

Baechu-jjim & gochu-gireum sauce 고추기름 배추찜

SERVES 4 AS A SIDE

Baechu-jjim is very simple: you just steam cabbage and put a dressing on top. We eat it at home when we don't have many ingredients and every time I think it's a perfect dish because it's humble but somehow luxurious, too. You can make the chilli oil ahead of time.

½ napa cabbage

CHILLI OIL
250 ml (8½ fl oz/1 cup)
   vegetable oil
2 spring onion (scallion) roots
2 spring onions (scallions),
   trimmed and thickly chopped
1 tablespoon julienned garlic
1 tablespoon julienned ginger
½ teaspoon whole black
   peppercorns
3 dried chillies
1 tablespoon gochugaru
   (Korean red chilli powder)

CHILLI GARLIC SAUCE
1 tablespoon minced garlic
1 red chilli, destemmed and
   minced
1 green chilli, destemmed
   and minced
125 ml (4 fl oz/½ cup) All-purpose
   soy sauce (page 44)
155 g (5½ oz/1 cup) chopped onion
45 g (1½ oz) chives
2 tablespoons Chilli oil (see above)
2 tablespoons Fermented fruit
   extract (page 20)
1 tablespoon Traditional
   persimmon vinegar (page 55),
   or apple-cider vinegar
1 teaspoon sesame oil

Start by making the chilli oil. Add 3 teaspoons of the vegetable oil to a frying pan over a high heat and stir-fry the spring onion roots, spring onion, garlic, ginger and peppercorns for 2 minutes.

Working quickly to prevent burning, add the remaining oil and, when it starts to boil, add the dried chillies and stir-fry over a low heat for 3 minutes.

Turn off the heat and allow the oil to cool for about 3 minutes (too hot, and the gochugaru will burn). Add the gochugaru, then leave the oil to cool completely.

Filter the oil through a fine-mesh sieve and transfer it to a dry bottle.

Cut the cabbage half into quarters and steam it for about 10 minutes. Part-fill a large saucepan with water and place a colander or sieve on top, making sure the water doesn't touch the base of the colander. Add the cabbage, cover with a lid and steam over a medium–high heat.

While the cabbage is steaming, make the chilli garlic sauce. Combine the garlic, chilli and soy sauce in a bowl and mix well. Add the remaining ingredients and stir to combine.

Remove the steamed cabbage and cut off the firmer stem end. Place the quarters neatly on a serving plate and sprinkle the prepared sauce over the top. Serve with a bowl of rice and your choice of protein.

MONKFISH FISH BALL SOUP

Agwi saengsun eomuktang 아귀 생선 어묵탕

SERVES 4

We've put this fish ball soup on the menu at CHAE. It's nice on a cold day because it's hot and a bit spicy. The main tip for success is to make the kelp stock the day before and cook it for at least 5 hours. If you can't find monkfish, you can replace it with another firm fish such as snapper; prawns (shrimp) are fine too.

FISHCAKE SOUP

2 litres (68 fl oz/8 cups) Anchovy & kelp broth (page 19)
100 g (3½ oz) daikon (white radish), destemmed, peeled and cut into 3 cm (1¼ in) slices
2 tablespoons Traditional Korean soup soy sauce (page 34)
1 tablespoon minced garlic
3 shiitake mushrooms, sliced
100 g (3½ oz) konjac noodles
2 red bullet chillies, destemmed and minced

AGWI BALL (MONKFISH FISH BALL)

200 g (7 oz) monkfish
200 g (7 oz) raw prawn (shrimp) meat
1 red chilli, destemmed, deseeded and minced
1 green chilli, destemmed, deseeded and minced
50 g (1¾ oz/1 cup) finely chopped chives
1 tablespoon minced garlic
1 teaspoon sesame oil

TO SERVE

½ teaspoon wasabi paste
1 tablespoon All-purpose soy sauce (page 44)
wasabi leaf (optional garnish)

Bring the anchovy and kelp broth to the boil in a large saucepan, then reduce the heat to medium and add the daikon. Simmer for 15–20 minutes, or until cooked through. Remove from the heat.

Meanwhile, for the agwi bowl, blend the monkfish and prawn meat in a food processor until you have a coarse paste. Place in a bowl and add the remaining ingredients along with a little salt and pepper. Use your hands to mix well. (If you like, you can cook a small portion of the mixture in a little oil in a frying pan to check the seasoning.)

Once the daikon is thoroughly cooked, season the soup with the soup soy sauce, garlic and salt. Add the mushroom and konjac to the soup and simmer over a low heat for about 5 minutes.

Working 1 teaspoon at a time, scoop up small portions of the fish mixture, shape into little balls, and drop into the soup. Add the chilli and simmer over a medium heat for 3 minutes, or until the fish balls are cooked. Season to taste with salt and freshly ground black pepper.

Place the soup in a bowl and serve with wasabi and all-purpose soy sauce.

STIR-FRIED BEEF GOCHUJANG

Sogogi yak gochujang 소고기 약고추장

SERVES 10 AS A SIDE

This is an elevated version of gochujang (Korean red chilli paste) with beef in it. It's a go-to multipurpose sauce that is great to have in the fridge. Throw a spoonful on rice with an egg or sesame oil and mix it together to make a quick bibimbap (see page 137). Serve it as a side dish with barbecue, or wrap it with rice in seaweed to make gimbap.

200 g (7 oz) minced (ground) beef
1 tablespoon sesame oil

MEAT SEASONING
1 tablespoon All-purpose soy
 sauce (page 44)
2 tablespoons cheongju
 (clear rice wine)
1 tablespoon Fermented fruit
 extract (page 20)

GOCHUJANG SEASONING
250 g (9 oz) gochujang (Korean
 red chilli paste)
2 tablespoons honey or jocheong
 (rice syrup)
3 tablespoons Fermented fruit
 extract (page 20)
2 tablespoons minced garlic
30 g (1 oz) pine nuts, or sunflower
 seeds or pepitas (pumpkin seeds)

Pat the beef with a paper towel to remove any blood.

Combine all the ingredients for the meat seasoning in a bowl, add the beef, mix well and leave to sit for 10 minutes.

Heat a dry frying pan over a medium heat and stir-fry the seasoned beef. Stir until the moisture is gone and there are no clumps. Add the sesame oil and continue stir-frying for 1 minute.

Add the gochujang and stir until the beef and gochujang are well mixed, then add all the remaining gochujang seasoning ingredients, except the pine nuts. Stir until smooth.

Lastly, add the pine nuts, increase the heat and boil until most of the liquid has evaporated, leaving a paste-like texture. Store in a sealed container or glass jar and use within 1 month.

BRAISED MACKEREL

Godeungeo jorim 고등어조림

SERVES 2

This spicy seafood dish is true Korean soul food. Radish and mackerel are both at their best in autumn, with deep flavours that work well together. Served with rice, this makes a simple and satisfying meal.

2 small mackerel
½ tablespoon coarse sea salt
500 ml (17 fl oz/2 cups) Anchovy
   & kelp broth (page 19)
¼ daikon (white radish),
   destemmed, peeled and cut
   into 2 cm (¾ in) slices
½ onion, sliced
1 spring onion (scallion), trimmed
   and chopped into 3 cm (1¼ in)
   pieces
1 red chilli, destemmed and sliced
   diagonally
20 g (¾ oz) chrysanthemum
   greens

SEASONING
2 tablespoons All-purpose soy
   sauce (page 44)
2 tablespoons gochugaru
   (Korean red chilli powder)
1 tablespoon minced garlic
1 tablespoon Fermented fruit
   extract (page 20)
1 tablespoon cheongju
   (clear rice wine)
1 teaspoon sesame oil
½ teaspoon salt
½ teaspoon pepper

Slit the mackerel lengthways down the belly and remove the guts. Wipe the cavity clean with a paper towel. Cut the two fillets off the mackerel, then cut each fillet in half crossways. Sprinkle with salt and refrigerate for about 2 hours.

Combine the seasoning ingredients in a bowl and mix well.

Cut each piece of daikon in half and add it to the anchovy and kelp broth in a saucepan. Increase the heat to high and bring the broth to a boil, then reduce the heat to low and part-cook the daikon, about 4 minutes.

Place the mackerel fillets in the broth, then cover evenly with the seasoning. Cover and simmer over a medium heat for 15 minutes, then add the onion, spring onion, chilli and chrysanthemum greens. Bring to the boil over a high heat and cook for another 2 minutes.

Serve with boiled rice and your preferred side dishes.

PORK KIMCHI STEW

Dwaejigogi kimchi-jjim 돼지고기 김치찜

SERVES 4

Kimchi-jjim is one of Korea's favourite dishes, a daily food that every family will prepare in a slightly different way. Even when the recipe is the same, everyone's kimchi is different so the dish will have its own character. I've even changed my recipe from my mum's version: she doesn't use stock. I'll eat this any day, any time with boiled rice.

500 g (1 lb 2 oz) pork spare ribs
500 g (1 lb 2 oz) Cabbage kimchi
  (page 158)
1 litre (34 fl oz/4 cups) Anchovy
  & kelp broth (page 19)
1 litre (34 fl oz/4 cups) kimchi juice
1 tablespoon gochugaru (Korean
  red chilli powder)

In a large stockpot, combine the pork spare ribs, whole cabbage kimchi, anchovy and kelp broth, and kimchi juice. Bring to the boil over a high heat.

Once boiling, reduce the heat to medium and add the gochugaru. Partially cover the stockpot and leave it to simmer for 2 hours or until the meat comes easily off the bone.

Serve the dish with rice and your favourite side dishes.

CHESTNUT RICE STONE BOWL WITH SEASONAL HERBS

Bahm Youngyangbap, namul 밤 영양밥, 나물

SERVES 4

Namul is a popular side dish that is nutritious and easy to prepare. It complements any meal and adds a nice touch to the dining table. You can serve it separately as a side dish alongside a bowl of rice, usually with your choice of protein. However, for a simple and quick meal, you can create your own bibimbap by mixing various namul with a spoonful of gochujang (Korean red chilli paste) and sesame oil.

300 g (10½ oz) multi-grain rice
300 g (10½ oz) white medium-grain rice
200 g (7 oz/1 cup) glutinous rice
5 chestnuts
10 lotus root slices
1 tablespoon pumpkin seeds
1 tablespoon sunflower seeds

Combine the multi-grain, white and glutinous rices together with the chestnuts and lotus root slices, then wash twice. Drain, add to a stone bowl and pour in enough water to cover the rice by 1 cm (½ in). Leave to soak for 1 hour.

Cover the stone bowl and bring to the boil over a high heat. Reduce the heat to medium and cook for 10 minutes. Reduce the heat to low and simmer for 5 minutes, then remove from the heat.

Once the rice is cooked, open the lid and mix thoroughly with a rice spoon.

BEAN SPROUT SIDE DISH

Sukju namul 숙주나물

300 g (10½ oz) bean sprouts
1 teaspoon coarse sea salt

SEASONING
15 g (½ oz) chopped spring onion (scallion)
½ tablespoon minced garlic
½ tablespoon fine sea salt
1 teaspoon sesame oil
1 tablespoon Fermented fruit extract (page 20)
1 teaspoon ground sesame seeds, plus extra to serve

Wash the bean sprouts under cold running water and drain in a colander.

Bring a saucepan of salted water to the boil and blanch the bean sprouts for 20 seconds. Immediately drain and rinse under cold running water.

Using your hands, squeeze as much water out of the bean sprouts as possible. Add all the seasoning ingredients and mix well. Serve on a plate and sprinkle with ground sesame seeds.

continued ...

CHRYSANTHEMUM SIDE DISH

Ssukat namul 쑥갓나물

300 g (10½ oz) chrysanthemum
  greens (available at Asian
  grocers)
1 teaspoon coarse sea salt
ground sesame seeds, to serve

SEASONING
15 g (½ oz) chopped spring onion
  (scallion)
½ tablespoon minced garlic
½ tablespoon fine sea salt
1 tablespoon perilla oil (available
  at Asian grocers)
1 tablespoon Fermented fruit
  extract (page 20)

Wash the chrysanthemum greens under cold running water and
drain in a colander.

Bring a saucepan of salted water to the boil over a high heat and
blanch the chrysanthemum greens for 20 seconds. Immediately
drain and rinse under cold running water.

Using your hands, squeeze as much water out of the chrysanthemum
as possible. Add all the seasoning ingredients and mix well. Serve on
a plate and sprinkle some ground sesame seeds on top.

SHIITAKE MUSHROOM SIDE DISH

Pyogo beosut namul 표고 나물 버섯

300 g (10½ oz) dried shiitake
  mushrooms
1 tablespoon vegetable oil
1 tablespoon chopped spring
  onion (scallion)
ground sesame seeds, to serve

SEASONING
1 teaspoon minced garlic
1 tablespoon Traditional Korean
  soup soy sauce (page 34)
½ tablespoon perilla oil
  (available at Asian grocers)
1 tablespoon perilla seed powder
  (available at Asian grocers)

Soak the shiitake mushrooms in a bowl of warm water for 1 hour.

Drain, then use your hands to squeeze out as much water as
possible from the mushrooms.

Remove the stems and slice the mushroom caps.

Prepare the seasoning by mixing all the ingredients in a bowl.
Add the sliced mushroom caps and mix well.

Heat the vegetable oil in a frying pan over a medium heat and
stir-fry the seasoned mushrooms for 4 minutes. Garnish with
the spring onion and ground sesame seeds and serve.

DRIED ZUCCHINI SIDE DISH

Hobakgoji namul 호박고지 나물

100 g (3½ oz) dried zucchini
    (courgette; available from
    Asian grocers)
1 tablespoon vegetable oil
125 ml (4 fl oz/½ cup) Anchovy
    & kelp broth (page 19)
2 tablespoons chopped spring
    onion (scallion)
1 teaspoon sesame oil
ground sesame seeds, to serve

SEASONING
2 tablespoons Traditional Korean
    soup soy sauce (page 34)
1 tablespoon perilla seed powder
    (available at Asian grocers)
1 teaspoon minced garlic
½ tablespoon perilla oil
    (available at Asian grocers)

Soak the dried zucchini in a bowl of cold water for 1 hour, then drain and squeeze out any excess water with your hands.

Combine all the seasoning ingredients in a bowl. Add the soaked zucchini and mix well.

Heat the vegetable oil in a frying pan over a medium heat and stir-fry the zucchini for 1 minute.

Add the anchovy and kelp broth, stir, then simmer until it has reduced down to 1 tablespoon of liquid. Transfer to a serving bowl and garnish with the spring onion, sesame oil and sesame seeds.

SPINACH SIDE DISH

Sigeumchi namul 시금치 나물

120 g (4½ oz) English spinach
1 teaspoon coarse sea salt
1 teaspoon ground sesame seeds

SEASONING
30 g (1 oz/¼ cup) chopped
    spring onion (scallion)
1 teaspoon fine sea salt
1 teaspoon minced garlic
½ tablespoon sesame oil
1 teaspoon ground sesame seeds
½ tablespoon Fermented fruit
    extract (page 20)

Prepare the spinach. Trim the root by scraping with a knife, then cut the bunch in half lengthways.

Bring a saucepan of water to the boil with the salt over a high heat. Blanch the spinach for about 30 seconds, then remove and immediately plunge into a bowl of iced water to stop the cooking process.

Drain, then, using your hands, squeeze as much water out of the spinach as possible. Add all the seasoning ingredients and mix well.

Transfer the spinach to a serving plate and garnish with the ground sesame seeds.

RICE CAKE WITH BEEF SPARE RIB SOUP
Galbitang tteokguk 갈비탕 떡국

It's a Korean tradition to enjoy this soup at Seollal, a national holiday marking the Korean New Year, which is calculated according to a lunar calendar. There's a Korean saying that when you have a bowl of tteokguk, you turn one year older. It's related to the Korean aging systems: everyone is considered one year old when they are born, and their age goes up on New Year's Day. We still celebrate the day we were born but it isn't when we turn a year older. That system lasted until 2023 when 'Korean Age' fell into line with 'International Age'.

2 kg (4 lb 6 oz) beef spare ribs
600 g (1 lb 5 oz) tteokguk rice
  cakes
2 tablespoons Traditional Korean
  soup soy sauce (page 34)

EGG GARNISH
½ teaspoon vegetable oil
2 eggs
1 pinch fine sea salt

TOPPINGS
2 eggs
5 g (⅛ oz) chopped spring onion
  (scallion)
1 piece of roasted seaweed,
  cut into strips

Place the beef in a bowl of cold water and soak for 2 hours to remove the blood, then drain.

Bring a stockpot of water to the boil and blanch the beef ribs for 10 minutes, then remove and rinse under cold running water. Trim any fat or impurities from the ribs.

Place the beef ribs in a stockpot of clean water and bring to the boil over a high heat. Reduce the heat to medium, half-cover the pot with the lid and simmer for 2 hours. Skim any fat that rises to the surface during cooking.

Separate the egg yolks and whites and remove the egg chalaza. Beat the egg yolks with a pinch of salt without creating foam.

Heat a frying pan over a low heat and rub the oil over the base of the pan with a paper towel. Spread the beaten yolk out in the pan and cook slowly for 2–3 minutes. Once one side is cooked, flip the egg and cook for another 2 minutes. Remove from the pan and set aside, then beat the egg whites and cook in the same way.

Once the egg is completely cooled, cut into 3 cm (1¼ in) pieces. Overlay the egg pieces and cut them into thin strips. Separate the yolk and white, ready to garnish.

Strain the broth through a sieve into a clean stockpot, add the rice cake and bring back to the boil. Add the soup soy sauce and cook for 5 minutes.

Once the rice cake floats to the surface, ladle the soup into serving bowls and garnish with the toppings in this order: meat, egg and spring onion. Season to taste with salt and pepper, sprinkle with the roasted seaweed and serve with kimchi.

PEAR GINGER TEA

Bae saenggang cha 배 생강차

SERVES 15

We make the most of autumn pears for this tea. It's a great drink for cool weather because it tastes warm and hearty and has medicinal properties.

When I was younger and caught a cold or experienced a sore throat, my mum would prepare this pear ginger tea, which always worked like a charm. The fiery ginger kept me warm and eased the discomfort in my throat. Pears, an excellent source of fibre, have a high water content that kept me hydrated. Their natural sweetness added a nice touch, making the tea even more enjoyable.

4 jujubes, deseeded
50 g (1¾ oz) cinnamon stick
2 nashi pears, peeled, cored and cut into 8 pieces
200 g (7 oz) ginger, peeled and thinly sliced
1 handful of spring onion (scallion) roots
200 g (7 oz) honey or brown sugar

Wash the jujubes and cinnamon sticks.

Place all the ingredients, except the honey, in a pressure cooker with 4 litres (135 fl oz/16 cups) water and boil over a medium heat. Once the cooker whistles, continue to boil for 5 minutes, then reduce the heat to low and simmer for another 10 minutes. Remove from the heat and, once the steam has been released, open the lid.

Strain the liquid through a fine-mesh sieve into a saucepan, discarding the solids. Add the honey and bring to the boil over a medium heat. Boil for 10 minutes, then remove from the heat and leave to cool.

Once cool, pour the tea into a container, seal and store in the fridge for up to 4 days.

To serve, reheat the tea on the stove or in a microwave until hot.

ORANGE EXTRACT SHAVED ICE

Orange balyho aek bingsu 오렌지 발효액 빙수

This is another dish that makes the most of autumn pears, this time in a shaved ice dessert. It's not a traditional dish but was something I invented for the restaurant. Seasoning with olive oil isn't a Korean technique but it works well. Use high-quality, fresh olive oil for the best flavour.

arils of ¼ pomegranate
4 tablespoons good-quality
    extra-virgin olive oil

FROZEN MILK
500 ml (17 fl oz/2 cups) full-cream
    (whole) milk, or milk of your
    choice
80 ml (2½ fl oz/⅓ cup) fermented
    orange extract (see page 20)

PEAR PICKLE
½ nashi pear, peeled and cored
1 tablespoon Traditional
    persimmon vinegar (page 55),
    or apple-cider vinegar
1 tablespoon fermented orange
    extract (see page 20)

Make the frozen milk by mixing the milk and fermented orange extract in a container, then freeze well.

Prepare the pear pickle. Use a mandoline to slice it thinly and place in a container. Mix the vinegar and fermented orange extract in a bowl, then drizzle this over the pear. Leave the pear to soak for about 10 minutes in the fridge.

Use an ice shaver to finely shave the frozen milk into a serving dish, then neatly arrange the pickled pears on top.

Top with the pomegranate arils, then drizzle with the olive oil.

TRADITIONAL KOREAN RICE DOUGHNUT
Gaeseong juak 개성주악

MAKES 20

Named 'juak' after the shape of a pebble, this traditional Korean dessert is a perfect combination of chewy, sticky rice bathed in jocheong (rice syrup). In the past, Gaeseong Juak was an essential dessert for special guests and wedding ceremonies. Today, it's a steady seller at Korean dessert cafes and has actually become somewhat trendy.

This is much easier to make than traditional Korean honey cookies but you do have to make the fermented rice syrup. The yeast in makgeolli (cloudy rice wine) kicks off the ferment, so make sure you buy raw makgeolli to achieve the correct result.

2 litres (68 fl oz/8 cups) vegetable oil, for deep-frying

RICE SYRUP EXTRACT
250 ml (8½ fl oz/1 cup) Fermented fruit extract (page 20)
250 ml (8½ fl oz/1 cup) jocheong (rice syrup)
20 g (¾ oz) ginger, peeled and cut into chunky pieces
3 g (⅙ oz) salt

RICE SYRUP WATER
35 ml (1¼ fl oz) jocheong (rice syrup)
1 tablespoon water

GAESEONG JUAK
300 g (10½ oz) glutinous rice flour
1 pinch fine sea salt
30 ml (1 fl oz) makgeolli (cloudy rice wine)
45 ml (1½ fl oz) Rice syrup water (see above)

To make the rice syrup extract, put all the ingredients in a saucepan and bring to the boil over a high heat. When the extract boils, reduce the heat to low and simmer for 15–20 minutes until the extract reduces to the consistency of honey. Gently skim off any foam that rises to the surface. Remove from the heat and leave to cool to room temperature.

Prepare the rice syrup water by combining the jocheong with the water in a saucepan and bringing to the boil. Remove from the heat.

For the Gaeseong juak, sift the rice flour into a bowl. Add the salt and makgeolli, bring together into a dough, then turn it out onto your kitchen bench. Knead, adding the hot rice syrup water, 1 tablespoon at a time, until the dough is smooth and no longer leaves a residue on your hands.

Take 15 g (½ oz) of the dough and shape it into a ball. Form a dent in the middle of the ball with the thick end of a chopstick. (If the dent is too small it will disappear when fried, so make sure it's about 1 cm/½ in wide to start with.)

Heat enough oil for deep-frying in a large saucepan over a medium heat. When the temperature reaches 85°C (185°F) on a cooking thermometer, add the doughnuts, working in two batches. Fry the doughnuts slowly for about 10 minutes, ensuring they don't stick together and flipping halfway through to ensure they are brown on both sides.

continued ...

When the doughnuts float to the surface of the oil, increase the heat until the oil temperature is 150°C (302°F) and continue frying until golden.

Place the fried doughnuts on a baking tray and leave to cool at room temperature.

Once cool, traditionally these doughnuts are left in the rice syrup extract to soak for approximately 12 hours. Then they are placed on a wire rack to strain for another 12 hours. However, if you prefer a fresh, crispy doughnut with a light coating, you can simply dip them in the extract and enjoy straight away.

겨울

Gyeo-wool

WINTER

CABBAGE KIMCHI
158

WHITE KIMCHI
162

RADISH KIMCHI IN
CHILLED DASHI BROTH
166

KIMCHI PANCAKES
169

RAW CRAB MARINATED
IN SPICY CHILLI SAUCE
& SOY SAUCE
172

FERMENTED SOYBEAN
STEW
178

ADZUKI BEAN
PORRIDGE
181

PUMPKIN
PORRIDGE
182

TOFU
185

TOFU HOT POT
188

TOFU, MUSHROOM &
PERILLA SEED
PORRIDGE
191

GROUND SOYBEAN
STEW WITH PORK
192

BOILED PORK
195

STEAMED CHICKEN
WITH CRISPY RICE CRUST
198

STEAMED PEAR
201

MANDARIN PEEL TEA
202

LEMON, GINGER
& FERMENTED
SWEETENER TEA
203

AUTUMN AND ITS FLOW INTO WINTER IS A BUSY TIME IN THE
TRADITIONAL KOREAN KITCHEN. IN AUTUMN WE HARVEST
FRUITS, VEGETABLES AND BEANS AND DRY THEM, READY
FOR WINTER FERMENTING PROJECTS. IN WINTER, MY MUM
WOULD ALSO PLANT RADISH, CABBAGE AND CHINESE
CABBAGE (WOMBOK), THEN HARVEST IT FOR MAKING KIMCHI,
A KEY SEASONAL TRADITION THAT MAKES ME THINK OF COLD
FINGERS AND TOES AS WE WORKED TOGETHER IN THE SNOW.
IT WAS CHILLY BUT SATISFYING: WE KNEW WE COULD RELY
ON PRESERVED FOODS THROUGH THE COLD MONTHS.

WINTER IS ALSO A TIME TO LAY THE GROUNDWORK FOR OTHER
CONDIMENTS, SUCH AS THE FERMENTED FRUIT EXTRACT (PAGE 20)
I USE IN SO MANY RECIPES AS A NATURAL SWEETENER. WE DO
EAT A LOT OF WARM SOUPS AND KIMCHI IN WINTER, BUT WE EAT
THEM IN SUMMER TOO: KOREAN LORE TELLS US THAT IT'S ALSO
GOOD TO EAT WARM FOODS WHEN OUR BODIES ARE WARM.
BASICALLY, EVERY SEASON IS SOUP SEASON!

CABBAGE KIMCHI
Baechu kimchi 배추김치

SERVES 10 AS A SIDE

I was once asked by a magazine reporter, 'Why is kimchi important to Koreans?' The question is simple but the answer is enormous, encompassing a huge narrative and a raft of memories that carry me from my childhood all the way to now, to the home I share with my husband Yoora and dog Haru in Cockatoo, outside Melbourne.

Kimchi is important like air is important. More than a foundation of our cuisine and a must with every meal, it's an accompaniment for our lives, threaded into daily and yearly rhythms. It wasn't until I'd been living in Australia for 10 years that I started properly making kimchi again. It was one of the things that set me on the path to cooking Korean food. Kimchi has been a touchstone, full of meaning for me forever.

My mother is the first child in her family and, as such, it's her responsibility to make lots and lots of kimchi to share with her relatives. I remember cabbages stacked in every corner of the kitchen in the depths of winter, when the temperature could be as cold as minus 20°C (minus 4°F). It was a feature of my childhood: a three-day kimchi immersion with aunties and neighbours and 500 cabbages every November or December. Of these hundreds of cabbages, we would keep only 10: the rest were distributed to family and neighbours.

There are endless memories associated with kimchi, both from Korea and my new home.

I remember an inflatable kids' swimming pool in the backyard filled with bright-red kimchi seasoning.

My mother and the aunties – I remember them talking softly and making light jokes.

I would get water, run errands, salt the cabbage. To be honest, I didn't love it, but looking back now makes me very nostalgic.

I remember my grandmother's crooked fingers elegantly tearing kimchi for my bowl of rice.

The familiar pungent smell of kimchi hits me every time I open the fridge – Koreans often have a separate kimchi fridge because the aroma is so powerful.

I think of my husband, who likes the crispy stems of the kimchi and my natural act of love to eat the outer leaves.

I can't help but remember my childhood with kimchi every time my mother visits me. She visits in winter, makes kimchi with me, and when she leaves, she leaves her kimchi. I see the kimchi, eat the kimchi, enjoy the kimchi but I am also filled with waves of emptiness that my mother has returned home. I feel her care, and also, her absence.

The preparation usually takes about 24 hours, so please allow yourself approximately two days to make kimchi.

2 napa cabbages

250 g (9 oz) coarse sea salt

½ daikon (white radish), peeled
and julienned

200 g (7 oz) spring onions
(scallions), trimmed and cut
into 3–4 cm (1¼–1½ in) lengths

200 g (7 oz) mustard greens,
cut into 3–4 cm (1¼–1½ in)
lengths

SEASONING

120 g (4½ oz) Glutinous rice paste
(page 21)

15 g (½ oz/¼ cup) dried anchovies

80 g (2¾ oz/½ cup) minced garlic

1 tablespoon minced ginger

½ pear or apple, cored

3 tablespoons aekjeot (fish sauce)

3 tablespoons jeotgal (page 51)

3 tablespoons Fermented fruit
extract (page 20)

250 g (9 oz/1 cup) gochugaru
(Korean red chilli powder)

3 tablespoons salted shrimp

SALTING

Trim the stem end of the cabbages crossways and remove any discoloured and damaged outer leaves.

Score a 5 cm (2 in) deep cross into the core.

Put your thumb between the cuts and slowly pull apart the cabbage lengthways into two pieces.

Prepare a bowl of saltwater by mixing the sea salt with 1.25 litres (42 fl oz/5 cups) water. The water to salt ratio should be 5:1.

Briefly immerse the cabbage halves in the saltwater, then remove.

Sprinkle a handful of salt in between the layers of each cabbage half, rubbing it into the outer layers, too.

In a round plastic basin, stack the salted cabbage halves, cut surfaces facing up.

Set aside at room temperature for about 6 hours during the warmer months or 10 hours if the weather is cooler, until the cabbage stems bend smoothly.

WASHING AND DRAINING

Once the cabbage stems bend smoothly, rub any dirt or impurities off the cabbage halves with your hands. Some liquid will have collected in the basin at this point, and you can use this to rinse the cabbage halves.

Score the base of the core. Put your thumb in between the cuts and slowly pull apart the cabbage pieces in half lengthways. You should be left with eight quarters.

Fill a large bowl with clean water and dip the cabbage quarters into the water four or five times to remove the salt, discarding the water and refilling the bowl with clean water each time.

Stack the cabbage quarters, stems facing upward. Leave to drain for 12 hours.

continued …

SEASONING

Put all the seasoning ingredients except the gochugaru and salted shrimp in a blender and blitz until smooth.

Add the blended mixture, gochugaru, salted shrimp, radish and mustard greens to a large bowl and mix well.

Fill the cabbage quarters with the seasoning mixture, working from the stem end up and rubbing it into each leaf. Bring the leaves back together and squeeze tightly to re-form the cabbage. Use the outermost leaf and tightly wind it around the cabbage to hold all the leaves in place. This will ensure the kimchi ferments well.

Place the kimchi in a container, seal and leave to ferment at room temperature for approximately 24 hours in the winter and 12 hours in summer.

Transfer to the fridge and continue to ferment the kimchi for another 2 weeks before serving. Kimchi keeps indefinitely, with some people preferring the sour, tangy flavour of well-aged kimchi and others preferring the fresher flavour of a shorter ferment – it's really up to you. Store in a sealed container in the fridge and remove each portion as you need it.

1

2

3

4

5

6

7

8

9

WHITE KIMCHI
Baek-kimchi 백김치

'Baek' means white and baek kimchi is made without using gochugaru (Korean red chilli powder), keeping it pale in colour. Plain salted napa cabbages made up the original kimchi, dating back to at least the 1600s, before red chilli was readily available.

The refreshing taste and crunchy texture make this a good palate cleanser with greasy dishes such as beef ribs, bulgogi, barbecue or even sashimi.

2 napa cabbages
½ daikon (white radish), peeled and julienned
150 g (5½ oz) spring onions (scallions), trimmed and cut into 3 cm (1¼ in) lengths
150 g (5½ oz) mustard greens, washed and cut into 3 cm (1¼ in) lengths

SEASONING
250 g (9 oz/1 cup) Glutinous rice paste (page 21)
10 g (¼ oz/1 cup) thinly sliced dried chilli
125 ml (4 fl oz/½ cup) aekjeot (fish sauce)
3 tablespoons salted shrimp
3 tablespoons minced garlic
1 teaspoon minced ginger

Salt, wash and drain the cabbage leaves according to the recipe on page 158.

Mix all the seasoning ingredients in a bowl and fill the softened napa cabbage with the seasoning from the stem up. Bring the leaves back together and squeeze tightly to re-form the cabbage. Use the outermost leaf and tightly wind it around the cabbage to hold all the leaves in place. This will ensure the kimchi ferments well.

Place the kimchi in a container and leave to ferment at room temperature for approximately 24 hours in the winter and 12 hours in summer.

Transfer to the fridge and continue to ferment the kimchi for another 2 weeks before serving. Kimchi keeps indefinitely, with some people preferring the sour, tangy flavour of well-aged kimchi and others preferring the fresher flavour of a shorter ferment – it's really up to you. Store in a sealed container in the fridge and remove each portion as you need it.

Radish kimchi in chilled dashi broth (page 166)

RADISH KIMCHI IN CHILLED DASHI BROTH

Dongchimi 동치미

SERVES 20 AS A SIDE

Koreans often look to this radish kimchi as a health remedy. You can hear people speaking about it in old movies as a folk remedy for the carbon monoxide poisoning that was unfortunately quite common in the 1960s and 70s when many Korean homes were heated with coal burners. Perhaps the older generations believed that the slightly sour, teeth-tingling dongchimi broth helped to 'wake up' ill people. I can't speak to the science, but I do know that this kimchi in broth revives my appetite when I'm feeling unwell.

4 daikon (white radishes), trimmed and peeled
80 g (2¾ oz) coarse sea salt
250 ml (8½ fl oz/1 cup) Anchovy & kelp broth (page 19)
150 g (5½ oz/½ cup) Glutinous rice paste (page 21)
3 tablespoons Fermented fruit extract (page 20)
125 ml (4 fl oz/½ cup) soju
1 nashi pear, cored and quartered
5 dried red chillies
5 spicy green chillies, scored
80 g (2¾ oz) jujubes, deseeded
120 g (4½ oz) spring onions (scallions), trimmed
150 g (5½ oz) mustard greens

SPICE BAG
2 tablespoons minced garlic
2 tablespoons minced ginger
½ onion, peeled and sliced

Place the radishes in a container and rub with 2 tablespoons of the coarse salt. Cover with the lid and leave for 1–2 days. Toss gently halfway through.

Add 4 litres (135 fl oz/16 cups) water, the anchovy and kelp broth, glutinous rice paste, fruit extract, soju and the remaining coarse salt, or to taste. (It is best to salt dongchimi generously, as it helps to preserve it. If the broth becomes too salty for you, just add some more water before serving.)

Neatly place the pear, the dried and fresh chillies, jujubes, spring onion and mustard greens on top of the radish. Combine the spice bag ingredients in a piece of mesh cloth and secure with twine. Place on top of the greens, then add the anchovy broth. Weigh down with a clean heavy plate.

Cover the container and leave the dongchimi to ferment at room temperature for 2 days, then transfer to the fridge and store for up to 3 months, removing portions as desired.

KIMCHI PANCAKES
Kimchi-jeon 김치전

SERVES 4

I am not sure why, but most Koreans have jeon (pancakes) with makgeolli (cloudy rice wine) on rainy days. My mum is also fond of making jeon, especially when coming to the end of a batch of kimchi, because the sourness of well-aged kimchi works so well with pancakes.

There's also a tradition of jeon and makgeolli on the way to mountaintops. When I was a child, we would sometimes go to the mountains near my mum's place. On the road, there's a huge place for pancakes and rice wine. Wherever you have it, the combination of kimchi-jeon made with tangy kimchi and a bowl of icy cold makgeolli is an extraordinary flavour parade that you must try!

In 2019, Yoora and I visited the famous Gwangjang Market in Seoul, said to be the oldest market in Korea and very well known for its street food. All of a sudden, it rained.

We were enveloped by the sound of heavy rain and the white noise of shop owners and customers chatting. The smell of wet asphalt and the sounds of the market made us crave pancakes and makgeolli. We can't explain it, but it was very powerful.

Almost without thinking, we made our way to a stall and ordered a bowl of makgeolli and kimchi-jeon. When you tear the golden, freshly fried kimchi pancake apart with chopsticks, the fragrant steam that breaks through from between the layers is phenomenal. We poured the milky makgeolli into a battered brass bowl and gulped it down immediately. The bubbles tickled our throats as they made their way down. It was exhilarating, especially as the alcohol quickly and pleasantly warmed our bodies. Maybe we don't need to explain how essential this combination is: we just need to urge you to try it!

continued ...

250 g (9 oz/1 cup) Cabbage kimchi
(page 158), aged for 1–2 months
and chopped, plus some kimchi
juice
100 g (3½ oz) Korean-pancake mix
(available from Asian grocers)
100 g (3½ oz) Korean frying mix
(available from Asian grocers)
150 g (5½ oz) mixed seafood
1 tablespoon gochugaru
(Korean red chilli powder)
vegetable oil, for shallow-frying
1 red chilli, destemmed and sliced
diagonally

DIPPING SAUCE
2 tablespoons All-purpose
soy sauce (page 44)
2 tablespoons Traditional
persimmon vinegar (page 55),
or apple-cider vinegar
¼ tablespoon sesame oil

In a bowl, combine the chopped kimchi, Korean pancake and frying mixes, the seafood, gochugaru and add some salt. Slowly add just enough kimchi juice to make a smooth batter that easily runs off a spoon. If you don't have enough kimchi juice, top up with a little water. (If the batter is too thick, the jeon will become hard.)

Make the dipping sauce by combing all the ingredients in a bowl.

Heat a frying pan over a medium heat and add enough oil for shallow-frying. Using a ladle, spoon a thin layer of batter into the pan. (You should have enough batter for two large pancakes.) If the batter consistency is right, it should spread out evenly and easily in the pan. Kimchi-jeon is most delicious when you use a generous amount of oil for frying.

Cook for 4–5 minutes. When the outer edge becomes crisp and golden, flip the pancake over and cook the other side until crispy. Press down gently with your spatula to ensure the pancake crisps well all over.

Once the kimchi-jeon is crisp and evenly golden, remove it from the pan and keep warm while you cook the other pancakes. Repeat with the remaining batter, then serve the kimchi-jeon with a couple of pieces of sliced chilli in the centre and the dipping sauce on the side.

TIP
It is essential to control the heat when making jeon, and cooking over a medium–high heat will provide the best results. If the heat is too low, the batter will become runny, and it will burn if the heat is too high.

RAW CRAB MARINATED IN
SPICY CHILLI SAUCE & SOY SAUCE

Yangnyeom-gejang and ganjang-gejang
양념게장, 간장게장

SERVES 4 AS A SIDE

I took this marinated crab for granted when I was a child. It was always there in the fridge because it's a staple in my mum's part of Korea. Haenam in Jeollanam-do is my mother's hometown, but it's better known as 'ddang-kkeut maeul', which means 'village at the end of the earth'. Due to Haenam's proximity to the sea, jeotgal (salted seafood, see page 51) is a typical side dish, so perhaps that explains why we never ran out of it.

It was only when I decided to make gejang for Yoora that I asked my mother for the recipe and started to appreciate the hard work that goes into it. It's so labour intensive! I realised that my mum trimmed every crab leg and crushed them so they were easier for me to eat. Now I remove the sharp crab shell bumps one by one so Yoora won't be hurt by them. I break the shell so the crab isn't too hard to chew. As my fingers throb and become numb, I finally glimpse my mother's hardship and love behind a staple food I never thought about much.

Gejang has a nickname: 'bab-doduk', which means 'rice thief' but has the sense of 'appetite arouser' because, before you know it, your bowl of rice disappears. Whether you're eating the version with spicy chilli marinade or the rich, umami-loaded soy sauce marinade, you have no trouble finishing a bowl of freshly cooked steaming rice when you gently mix in the crab flesh.

PREPARATION AND CLEANING

To prepare your blue crabs, use a clean toothbrush or brush to scrub the shell and legs, then wash in clean water.

Turn the crab over, pull the apron from the body and discard.

Pull the abdomen from the body shell.

Gently pull and remove the foregut, which is located in the body shell close to the eyes. Next, carefully remove the gills.

Using scissors, cut off the antennae, eyes, mouth parts and the tips of the legs, which don't contain any meat.

Cut the body in half vertically, then halve each half again horizontally. You should have four pieces, plus the claws.

Cut the claws in half using a knife, then use one claw to remove the flesh inside the other claw, and vice versa. Remove the claw spikes with a knife, then gently break the claws.

Freeze the cleaned crabs for at least 30 minutes, but up to 1 hour.

1

2

3

4

CRABS IN SPICY CHILLI SAUCE

Yangnyeom gaejang 양념게장

2 blue crabs, cleaned
sesame seeds, to serve

MARINADE
80 ml (2½ fl oz/⅓ cup) All-purpose
    soy sauce (page 44)
5 garlic cloves, peeled
2.5 cm (1 in) piece of ginger,
    peeled
1 tablespoon sesame oil
½ onion, peeled
3 tablespoons gochugaru
    (Korean red chilli powder)

VEGETABLES
1 spring onion (scallion),
    trimmed and sliced
½ onion, sliced
1 red chilli, destemmed and sliced
1 green chilli, destemmed
    and sliced

Start with the marinade. Bring the soy sauce to the boil in a small saucepan over a high heat, then let it cool completely before preparing the crabs.

Put all the marinade ingredients except the gochugaru in a blender and blitz until smooth.

Thoroughly mix the marinade, gochugaru and slightly frozen crab (see page 172) in a bowl, then add the prepared vegetables.

Sprinkle with sesame seeds and eat within 4 days.

CRABS IN SOY SAUCE

Ganjang–gejang 간장게장

5 blue crabs, cleaned
sesame seeds, to serve

SOY SAUCE MARINADE
500 ml (17 fl oz/2 cups) All-purpose
    soy sauce (page 44)
250 ml (8½ fl oz/1 cup) Traditional
    Korean soup soy sauce
    (page 34)
250 ml (8½ fl oz/1 cup) soju
250 ml (8½ fl oz/1 cup) Fermented
    fruit extract (page 20)
50 g (1¾ oz) shiitake mushrooms
30 g (1 oz) garlic cloves, peeled
5 dried red bullet chillies
½ onion
½ apple or pear
20 g (¾ oz) piece of ginger, peeled
1 spring onion (scallion) root
5 × 5 cm (2 × 2 in) piece of
    dried kelp

VEGETABLES
1 spring onion (scallion),
    trimmed and sliced
½ onion, sliced
1 red chilli, destemmed and
    chopped into thirds
1 green chilli, destemmed and
    sliced
5 garlic cloves
1 lemon, sliced

Start this recipe 5 days before you plan to serve it.

Combine all the marinade ingredients in a stockpot with 1 litre
(34 fl oz/4 cups) water and boil over a high heat. Once boiling,
cover with a lid, reduce the heat to low and simmer for 20 minutes.

Strain the marinade through a sieve into a container and leave it
to cool completely. Discard the solids.

To prepare your crabs, use a clean toothbrush or other small brush
to scrub the shells and legs, then wash them in clean water.

Unlike the spicy chilli crabs opposite, the crabs are marinated
whole in this recipe. Place the whole crabs in a container with
the abdomens facing downwards so they fit snugly, minimising
any gaps.

Pour the cooled marinade over the crab to fully submerge.

Cover with the lid and refrigerate for 24 hours.

After 24 hours, remove the crab to a clean container and strain the
marinade into a clean saucepan. Add 125 ml (4 fl oz/½ cup) water
to the marinade and bring to the boil over a medium heat. Once
boiling, remove from the heat and set aside to cool completely.
Once fully cooled, pour back over the crab. Refrigerate for another
24 hours.

Repeat this process one more time. Remove the crab to a clean
container and strain the the marinade into a clean saucepan.
Add 60 ml (2 fl oz/¼ cup) water to the marinade and bring to the
boil over a medium heat. Once boiling, remove from the heat and
set aside to cool completely. Once cooled, pour back over the crab
and add the vegetables. Cover with a lid and keep in the fridge for
3 days to age.

Store in the fridge for up to 1 week, removing portions as desired.
Sprinkle with sesame seeds before serving.

Crabs in soy sauce (page 175)

FERMENTED SOYBEAN STEW
Cheonggukjang-jjigae 청국장찌개

SERVES 2-3

One day towards the beginning of our relationship, Yoora had a homesick craving for cheonggukjang stew made by his mum. 'I want to travel to Korea for it,' he said. I was determined to comfort him the best way possible, so I made my way to a Korean food store to buy a packet of cheonggukjang (stinky fermented soybean). I made cheonggukjang stew with extra-fermented kimchi, pork and zucchini (courgette). The thick and hearty soup with spicy gochugaru was the perfect way to soothe his nostalgia.

Not everyone will be soothed by this stew! It's notorious for its smell, which some people compare to wet socks. When Yoora moved to Canada for high school and made it one day, the people he was staying with reported a mysterious unpleasant odour. Once you acquire the taste though, you will crave it, too.

1 tablespoon sesame oil
500 g (1 lb 2 oz) Cabbage kimchi (page 158), aged for 1–2 months and cut into bite-sized pieces
300 g (10½ oz) pork fillet (tenderloin), cut into bite-sized pieces
200 g (7 oz) Sticky fermented soybean paste (page 47)
1 tablespoon Traditional Korean soybean paste (page 34)
1 tablespoon gochugaru (Korean red chilli powder)
½ tablespoon minced garlic
150 g (5½ oz) medium-firm tofu, cut into bite-sized pieces
1 zucchini (courgette), cut into bite-sized pieces

Heat the oil in a saucepan over a medium heat and stir-fry the kimchi for 1 minute until lightly cooked.

Add the pork and continue to stir-fry for 4 minutes, then add 2 litres (68 fl oz/8 cups) water and bring to the boil.

Once boiling, add the cheonggukjang and soybean paste. Mix well to prevent any clumps.

Add the gochugaru, garlic and tofu. Reduce the heat to low and simmer until the ingredients have softened.

Just before serving, add the zucchini, bring back to the boil, then switch off the heat, and it's ready to serve with rice.

ADZUKI BEAN PORRIDGE

Dongji patjuk 동지팥죽

SERVES 4

Since ancient times, Koreans have believed that red beans have positive energy and drive away evil spirits and ghosts. The winter solstice (22–23 December) is thought to have abundant negative energy, so on this longest night of the year, it's traditional to eat red bean porridge to protect people and homes. This version of red bean porridge includes sticky rice balls, which represent the rebirth of the sun, again driving away evil spirits.

Even if you're not superstitious, you can enjoy red bean porridge as a simple meal that is very nutritious and easy to digest.

500 g (1 lb 2 oz) adzuki beans
100 g (3½ oz/½ cup) white medium-grain rice
3 tablespoons Fermented fruit extract (page 20)
1 tablespoon coarse sea salt
½ teaspoon pine nuts

SAEAL (STICKY RICE BALLS)
100 g (3½ oz) glutinous rice flour
1 pinch of fine sea salt
1 tablespoon makgeolli (cloudy rice wine)
2 tablespoons hot water

Put the beans in a saucepan and cover with water. Bring to the boil over a high heat and cook for 5 minutes. Drain, then rinse the beans under cold running water. Set aside.

Transfer the beans to a stockpot and cover with 2 litres (68 fl oz/ 8 cups) water. Bring to the boil over a high heat, then reduce the heat to medium and simmer for 50 minutes until soft and the beans can be easily mashed between your fingers.

In the meantime, make the saeal. Mix the glutinous rice flour, pinch of salt and makgeolli using a wooden spoon. Add the hot water and continue mixing with a wooden spoon to avoid burning your hands. Once cooled a little, knead with your hands until the dough is smooth and no longer leaves a residue on your hands.

Cut and weigh the dough into 15 g (½ oz) pieces, then roll each piece into a ball with your hands. Set aside.

Add the cooked beans to a blender with 1.5 litres (51 fl oz/6 cups) water and blitz to a smooth texture.

Pour the bean mixture into a saucepan and bring to the boil over a medium heat. Drain the rice and add to the bean mixture. Continue to cook the porridge for about 10 minutes.

Bring 1 litre (34 fl oz/4 cups) water to the boil in a saucepan with a pinch of salt. Once boiling, add the prepared saeal and cook until they rise to the surface. Remove with a slotted spoon, then transfer to a colander and rinse under cold running water. Rinse the rice, then soak it in a bowl of water for 30 minutes.

Add the fermented fruit extract and salt to the porridge, then boil for another 15 minutes, or until the porridge thickens. Add the prepared saeal and boil for 5 more minutes, then switch off the heat. Serve the patjuk in a bowl with the pine nuts scattered on top.

PUMPKIN PORRIDGE

Hobakjuk 호박죽

SERVES 4

When I was young, my grandmother, who lived in the countryside, used to make pumpkin (winter squash) porridge in a large pot over an open fire. It's like a faded picture in my memory: my grandmother's back bending over, the long wooden spatula she used to scoop the bright-yellow pumpkin porridge, the sound of soup boiling and the spicy-sweet scent resonating through the kitchen.

At our restaurant, some customers told me the porridge reminded them of their hometowns. I wonder if my childhood memories permeated through the pumpkin porridge without me realising it.

In Korea, you can find many porridge restaurants, especially near hospitals. Because porridge is so easy to digest and universally enjoyed, it's something that people often bring with them when they visit a patient.

I use sweet kent (jap) pumpkin in this recipe because it's similar to Korean pumpkin.

¼ kent (jap) pumpkin
    (winter squash)
2 litres (68 fl oz/8 cups) full-cream
    (whole) milk
100 g (3½ oz/1 cup) walnuts,
    plus extra crushed walnuts
    to garnish
80 ml (2½ fl oz/⅓ cup) jocheong
    (rice syrup), or agave or maple
    syrup
½ tablespoon fine sea salt
1 teaspoon crushed pine nuts

SAEAL (STICKY RICE BALLS)
100 g (3½ oz) glutinous rice flour
pinch of salt
1 tablespoon makgeolli (cloudy
    rice wine)
2 tablespoons hot water

GLUTINOUS RICE WATER
2 tablespoons glutinous rice flour

Remove the skin and seeds of the pumpkin and cut the flesh into 5 cm (2 in) pieces.

Place the pumpkin in a pot with the milk and walnuts and bring to the boil over a high heat. Once boiling, reduce the heat to medium, cover with a lid and simmer for 25 minutes.

In the meantime, make the saeal.

Mix the glutinous rice flour, salt and makgeolli using a wooden spoon. Add the hot water and continue mixing with a wooden spoon to avoid burning your hands. Once cooled a little, knead with your hands until the dough is smooth and no longer leaves a residue on your hands.

Cut and weigh the dough into 15 g (½ oz) pieces, then roll each piece into a ball with your hands. Set aside.

Prepare the glutinous rice water by mixing the glutinous rice flour with 80 ml (2½ fl oz/⅓ cup) water in a small bowl.

Once the pumpkin is completely soft, drain, then transfer it to a blender and blitz until smooth. Pour the pumpkin purée into a saucepan and bring to a simmer over a low heat. Slowly add the glutinous rice water, mixing well with a spatula. Cover and simmer for about 10 minutes.

Bring 1 litre (34 fl oz/4 cups) salted water to the boil in a saucepan. Once boiling, add the prepared saeal and cook until they rise to the surface. Remove with a slotted spoon, then transfer to a colander and rinse under cold running water.

Just before serving, add the jocheong, salt and the saeal and bring to the boil for about 5 minutes to heat everything through.

Place in a serving bowl and top with pine nuts and walnuts to garnish.

TOFU
Dubu 두부

SERVES 2

Most Korean food is easy to make but the processes are long and you need to plan ahead. For example, the nigari (coagulant) that's used to make tofu is created by harvesting fresh sea salt. We put it in a big bag, snip the lower corners, and, after months (and years) the seawater slowly drips through and can be used to form tofu. Luckily, you can also purchase it in liquid or powder form.

Home-made tofu isn't very smooth and it's quite soft. You can press it to make it harder, or add more nigari as you make it.

We make this tofu to eat more or less straight away: my mum would use it in a stew, or we'd eat it as is with a spoon of soy sauce and sesame oil on top.

200 g (7 oz) soybeans
½ tablespoon perilla oil
   (available at Asian grocers)
1 teaspoon sea salt
1 teaspoon nigari solution
   (mixed with 2 tablespoons
   water)

Wash the soybeans and rinse them thoroughly two or three times.

Place in a bowl, cover with cold water and leave to soak for about 8 hours. Once soaked, the beans will weigh about 400 g (14 oz).

Drain the water from the soybeans and add them to a blender with double the weight of water, about 1 kg (2 lb 3 oz). Blitz until smooth (the smoother the soybeans, the more tofu you will get).

Pour the soybean purée into a cotton cloth, gather the corners and squeeze as much soymilk as you can through the cloth into a bowl.

Add 500 ml (17 fl oz/2 cups) water to the cloth, then gather the corners and squeeze again. (Keep the soy pulp for making Ground soybean stew with pork, page 192.) Store in the fridge for up to 3 days (or in the freezer for longer).

Transfer the soymilk to a large pot and simmer over a low heat for 15 minutes, skimming any foam that rises to the surface.

After 15 minutes, add the perilla oil and sea salt. (Perilla oil not only prevents foaming but also enhances the rich, savoury flavour.) Slowly add the nigari solution to the soymilk. Cover with a lid and simmer over the lowest possible heat for 5 minutes.

Check the clarity of the soymilk. If it is clear, then you can move on to the next step. Otherwise, make some more nigari solution by mixing ½ teaspoon nigari with 1 tablespoon water and add this. Repeat until you get clear soymilk.

Pour the curds into a tofu mould or fine-mesh sieve lined with a cotton cloth or muslin (cheesecloth). Fold the cloth over the tofu and place a flat, heavy object on top to weigh it down. If you want extra-firm tofu, leave the weight for about 1 hour. For medium–firm, leave it for 15–25 minutes.

1

2

3

4

5

6

7

8

9

10

11

12

TOFU HOT POT
Dubu-jeongol 두부전골

SERVES 4

Jeongol is a hearty Korean soup often enjoyed as a communal meal. Typically it includes a mixture of vegetables, mushrooms, seafood, meat and tofu all simmered in a flavourful savoury broth. The highlight of jeongol comes after the main meal is finished: rice is added to the leftover broth, seaweed and sesame oil are sprinkled on top, and the mixture is left to cook until a crust forms on the bottom. This delicious rice dish is a satisfying conclusion to a meal.

300 g (10½ oz) medium-firm Tofu (page 185)
1 potato, peeled and cut into 1 cm (½ in) slices
50 g (1¾ oz) enoki mushrooms
50 g (1¾ oz) shimeji mushrooms
4–5 shiitake mushrooms
½ onion, sliced
1–2 spring onions (scallions), trimmed and sliced diagonally
1 red bullet chilli, destemmed and sliced diagonally
2 litres (68 fl oz/8 cups) Anchovy & kelp broth (page 19)
1 teaspoon sesame oil
sesame seeds, to serve

SAUCE
80 ml (2½ fl oz/⅓ cup) All-purpose soy sauce (page 44)
2 tablespoons Traditional Korean soup soy sauce (page 34)
2 tablespoons Fermented fruit extract (page 20)
2 tablespoons gochugaru (Korean red chilli powder)
1 tablespoon minced garlic

Remove the excess water from the tofu (see page 185) and cut it into bite-sized pieces. Sprinkle with salt and let it sit for 10 minutes.

Make the sauce by combining all the ingredients in a bowl.

Place the sliced potato in the bottom of a shallow sauté pan and top with the tofu.

Add the prepared vegetables to the pan, then spread the sauce evenly over the ingredients. Add just enough of the anchovy and kelp broth to slightly submerge the tofu.

Cover with a lid and bring to the boil over a high heat, then reduce the heat to low and simmer for 15 minutes or until the soup thickens. Once the potatoes are fully cooked (test them by piercing with a knife), remove from the heat.

Serve, either straight from the pan or in individual serving bowls, topped with the sesame oil and sesame seeds.

TOFU, MUSHROOM & PERILLA SEED PORRIDGE
Dubu buhsut deulkkae juk 버섯들깨죽

SERVES 2

Perilla is a key food in Korean cuisine. We use its oil and a powder made from the seeds in this creamy, soupy porridge. The powder thickens the dish and has a strong, nutty flavour. Texture is a crucial component of this dish, and the mushrooms add their particular bite and mouthfeel too.

80 g (2¾ oz) medium-firm Tofu (page 185)
2 tablespoons vegetable oil
1 teaspoon perilla oil (available at Asian grocers)
15 g (½ oz) enoki mushrooms
15 g (½ oz) king oyster mushrooms, cut into bite-sized pieces
500 ml (17 fl oz/2 cups) Vegetable stock (see below)
1 tablespoon Traditional Korean soup soy sauce (page 34)
40 g (1½ oz/½ cup) perilla seed powder (available at Asian grocers)
1 spring onion (scallion), trimmed and sliced diagonally into 2 cm (¾ in) lengths

VEGETABLE STOCK
5 × 5 cm (2 × 2 in) piece of dried kelp
3 dried shiitake mushrooms

Remove the excess water from the tofu (see page 185) and cut it into bite-sized pieces. Sprinkle with salt and let it sit for 10 minutes.

Heat the vegetable oil in a frying pan over a medium heat and fry the tofu until golden brown on all sides.

To prepare the enoki mushrooms, trim the bottom 5 cm (2 in) from each and discard. Separate the mushroom strands into bite-sized pieces, then chop crossways into two or three pieces.

In the meantime, make the vegetable stock. Combine the kelp and shiitake mushrooms with 500 ml (17 fl oz/2 cups) water in a saucepan and boil over a medium heat for 10 minutes. Strain the stock into a clean container, discarding the kelp. Using your hands, squeeze as much liquid out of the shiitake mushrooms as possible, then slice.

Heat the perilla oil in a frying pan and stir-fry the enoki, king oyster and shiitake mushrooms over a medium heat for about 3 minutes. Add the soy sauce and continue to stir-fry.

Pour in the vegetable stock and bring to the boil, then add the perilla seed powder and tofu and boil for 5 minutes to heat through. Season to taste with salt.

Add the spring onion and boil for another 10 seconds, then remove from the heat, scoop into bowls and serve.

GROUND SOYBEAN STEW WITH PORK
Biji-jjigae 돼지고기 비지찌개

SERVES 2

This stew is a by-product of the tofu-making process, using up the soy pulp left over from making soymilk (see page 87). It has a very nutty flavour and can be eaten as a meal by itself or served with rice. I suggest using pork shoulder for this dish, but you can also use belly.

1 tablespoon vegetable oil
1 tablespoon sesame oil
200 g (7 oz) pork shoulder, trimmed and finely chopped
200 g (7 oz) Cabbage kimchi (page 158), aged for 1–2 months, chopped
1 tablespoon gochugaru (Korean red chilli powder)
750 ml (25½ fl oz/3 cups) Anchovy & kelp broth (page 19)
1 tablespoon salted shrimp
¼ onion, sliced
1 tablespoon minced garlic
300 g (10½ oz) soy pulp from making tofu (see page 185)
1 spring onion (scallion), trimmed and sliced diagonally
1 hot green chilli, destemmed and sliced diagonally
1 tablespoon Traditional Korean soup soy sauce (page 34)

Heat the vegetable and sesame oils in a saucepan over a high heat and brown the pork.

Add the kimchi and gochugaru and stir-fry for another 3 minutes. Add the anchovy and kelp broth and bring to the boil.

Once boiling, add the salted shrimp, onion and garlic and boil over a high heat for 3 minutes.

Add the prepared soy pulp, reduce the heat to low and simmer for 15 minutes.

Add the spring onion, green chilli and soup soy sauce and cook for another minute.

The stew is best served with steamed rice, but you can also enjoy it as a healthy, low-calorie meal without the rice.

BOILED PORK
Bossam 보쌈

SERVES 4

When we finish making kimchi, we eat it with this braised pork. It's a tradition to eat some fresh kimchi straight away, and the flavours all match really well. Other foods to enjoy with bossam include salted shrimp, oysters, musaengchae (spicy radish salad), the yellow inner leaves of salted cabbage and leafy vegetables. We usually drink makgeolli (cloudy rice wine) or soju to accompany our feast.

2 kg (4 lb 6 oz) piece of pork belly
fresh Cabbage kimchi (page 158),
    to serve

SSAMJANG DIPPING SAUCE
1 tablespoon Traditional Korean
    soybean paste (page 34)
1 tablespoon gochujang (Korean
    red chilli paste)
1 tablespoon sesame oil
½ tablespoon minced garlic
1 teaspoon ground sesame seeds

SALTED FISH SAUCE
2 tablespoons aekjeot (fish sauce)
½ tablespoon minced garlic
1 tablespoon minced red chilli
100 g (3½ oz) garlic chives,
    chopped

SUYUK SPICES
1 tablespoon Traditional Korean
    soybean paste (page 34)
60 ml (2 fl oz/¼ cup) soju
10 whole black peppercorns
3–5 garlic cloves, peeled
2 spring onions (scallions),
    trimmed and chopped into
    3–4 pieces
2.5 cm (1 in) piece of ginger

Heat a frying pan over a high heat and sear the pork belly on all sides to seal.

Prepare enough water in a large stockpot to cover the pork belly. Add the doenjang and stir to dissolve. Add the seared pork belly with the remaining suyuk spices and bring to the boil over a high heat.

Once the suyuk soup boils, reduce the heat to medium and simmer for about 1 hour.

Combine the ssamjang dipping sauce ingredients in a small bowl.

Mix the salted fish sauce ingredients in another bowl and set aside.

Once the meat is cooked to a soft texture, remove the belly and leave to cool on a tray. Cut the meat into 5 mm (¼ in) pieces, plate it neatly and serve with kimchi, ssamjang and the salted fish sauce.

TIP
Bossam is typically served with gutjuri (page 115) and mumallaengi (page 122). These accompaniments complement the rich savoury flavour of the bossam, adding freshness and crunch to each bite.

STEAMED CHICKEN WITH CRISPY RICE CRUST

Nurungji dak-samgye-tang 누룽지 삼계탕

SERVES 2

Korean dishes believed to have nourishing properties are known as boyangsik. They're prepared with ingredients considered to have health-promoting benefits, such as certain grains, vegetables and medicinal herbs, and are most often enjoyed when you need to replenish your energy or strengthen your body, such as after an illness or during the cold winter months.

Samgyetang, or chicken soup, is a typical example of boyangsik. This hearty and nutritious meal provides a balance of essential nutrients to support overall well-being.

1 × 1.35–1.45 kg (3–3 lb 3 oz) whole chicken, trimmed of excess fat
250 g (9 oz/1 cup) glutinous rice
120 g (4½ oz/1 cup) chopped spring onion (scallion)

KOREAN MEDICINAL HERBS
1 packet of Samgyetang soup base (available at Korean grocers)
60 g (2 oz) garlic cloves, peeled
salt and pepper, to taste

Stuff the cavity with the soup base contents and half the garlic cloves, then close the opening with toothpicks.

Rinse the glutinous rice twice, then spread it in the base of a pressure cooker and place the prepared chicken on top.

Scatter the remaining garlic cloves around the chicken, then add just enough water to submerge the chicken.

Boil on high until the pressure cooker starts to whistle, then leave it on high heat for another 2 minutes before reducing to medium and cooking for another 15 minutes. Turn off the heat and leave it to sit and simmer in the residual heat for 10 minutes before opening.

Open the pressure cooker and transfer the chicken to a bowl. Remove the liquid, add half to the bowl with the chicken and reserve the other half to cook the rice.

Before serving, season the meat and soup to taste with salt and pepper. In traditional fashion, the chicken is presented whole, allowing individuals to personally shred the meat from the bones.

Turn the cooker to low heat and leave the rice for 15 minutes to scorch on the bottom.

Once the bottom of the rice turns golden, pour the reserved soup back into the pressure cooker and boil the porridge for 20 minutes, or until thickened to a porridge-like texture. Season to taste with salt and serve with the spring onion.

STEAMED PEAR

Baesook 배숙

SERVES 5

2 teaspoons bicarbonate of soda
(baking soda)
5 nashi pears
1.5–2 cm (½–¾ in) piece of ginger,
sliced into thin strips
1 jujube, deseeded and thinly
sliced
peel of ½ lemon, julienned
2 tablespoons jocheong
(rice syrup)
10 g (¼ oz) pine nuts

This winter dessert is good for sore throats and colds thanks to its medicinal combination of pear, ginger and jujube.

Rub the bicarbonate of soda on the skin of the pears to wash them.

Cut 1 cm (½ in) off the top of each pear to use later as a lid.

Use a small spoon to scoop out the pear flesh, leaving only about 5 mm (¼ in) around the edge. Remove the seeds and place the flesh in a bowl with the ginger, jujube and julienned lemon peel.

Add 1 tablespoon of the jocheong and mix well, then fill the pear with the mixture. Carefully pour the remaining jocheong on top of the stuffing, scatter a few pine nuts on top and cover each pear with its lid.

Place the pear in a steamer, cover and steam over a medium heat for about 30 minutes. Or you can use the double-boiler method: set a colander over a saucepan of simmering water, making sure the water doesn't touch the base of the colander. Add the pear, cover with a lid and steam over a medium heat for 30 minutes.

This dish is most delicious when served hot, but you can cool it down in the refrigerator and serve it later as a snack, too.

MANDARIN PEEL TEA
Jinpicha 진피차

MAKES 150 G (5½ OZ)

You need to plan ahead for this one because it's best when aged for three years, though you can start using it after one year. It's refreshing, floral, has a lovely orange colour and has many medicinal uses, too: it's good for the respiratory and digestive systems.

We wash the fruit with bicarbonate of soda (baking soda) to make it extra clean.

½ tablespoon bicarbonate of soda
   (baking soda)
20 organic mandarins

Rub the bicarbonate of soda and some salt into the skin of the mandarins to wash them.

Peel the mandarins and slice the skin into thin strips.

Place the mandarin peel in a frying pan over a medium–low heat and stir for 5 minutes to remove the moisture. Watch it closely to ensure it doesn't burn.

Transfer the peel to a bamboo tray to cool. During cooling, rub the peel lightly between your hands to enhance the scent and flavour.

Repeat the heating and drying process about five times to completely remove the moisture. The more you repeat the process, the better your finished tea will taste.

Place the dried peel in an airtight container and store in cool, dry place. You can enjoy it right away, but the flavour and health benefits improve with longer aging. Ideally, leave it to age for 1–3 years.

Feel free to adjust the tea and water quantities to achieve your preferred tea strength and serving size. As a general guideline, steeping 3 g (⅛ oz) of tea in 250 ml (8½ fl oz/1 cup) hot water for 3–5 minutes will make a suitable strength for a single serving of tea.

LEMON, GINGER & FERMENTED SWEETENER TEA

Bae saenggang hyoso cha 배 생강 효소 차

MAKES 2 LITRES
(68 FL OZ/8 CUPS)

This is one of my favourite winter drinks. It's sweet, sour, refreshing and spicy and, when we serve it at CHAE, it's always one of the most popular beverages. You can enjoy it either hot or cold. It's really good for digestion and sore throats.

300 g (10½ oz) ginger, peeled and finely grated
600 ml (20½ fl oz) lemon juice
1 litre (34 fl oz/4 cups) Fermented fruit extract (page 20)

Start this recipe 1 week before you want to serve it.

Mix the ginger and lemon juice in a container, cover and leave in the fridge to ferment for 1 week.

After a week, filter the mixture through a mesh cloth into a clean container.

Mix the fermented fruit extract with the ginger–lemon juice, then pour into a bottle, seal and refrigerate for 2 weeks to age further before serving.

Dilute 100 ml (3½ fl oz) of the juice concentrate with 100 ml (3½ fl oz) hot water, or using sparkling water for a refreshing alternative. You can also use the juice concentrate in various recipes, including in a salad dressing. Feel free to adjust the concentrate to water ratio according to your preference.

TIP
Store the ginger and lemon pulp in a vacuum-pack bag and freeze to use in other recipes, such as the All-purpose soy sauce (page 44).

Mandarin peel tea (page 202)

Lemon, ginger & fermented sweetener tea (page 203)

봄

Bom

SPRING

DICED RADISH KIMCHI
212

MUGWORT KIMCHI
213

SPINACH KIMCHI
213

PICKLED GARLIC
SCAPES
216

GOCHUJANG
PICKLED GARLIC
217

PICKLED GREEN CHILLI
WITH SOYBEAN PASTE
220

BRAISED BEEF & EGGS
IN SOY SAUCE
222

MARINATED EGGS
IN SOY SAUCE
225

WATER CELERY &
BULGOGI HOT POT
226

KOREAN KNIFE-CUT
NOODLES WITH
FRESH PIPIS
228

SPICY BEEF SOUP
233

BRAISED SNAPPER
234

COD IN MUSSEL BROTH
237

BEAN SPROUT
STEAMED RICE WITH
SOY SAUCE DRESSING
239

SEASONAL SEASONED
GREENS & VEGETABLES
242

FERMENTED RICE
BEVERAGE
244

SPRING IS A JOYFUL SEASON IN KOREA AS WE ALL EMERGE
FROM THE BITTER WINTER AND START TO ENJOY THE FRESH
HERBS AND VEGETABLES OF THE NEW SEASON. SOME
SEAFOOD IS ALSO OF EXTRAORDINARY QUALITY AT THIS
TIME OF YEAR AS THE WATERS SLOWLY START TO WARM:
PIPIS (VONGOLE) ARE ONE EXAMPLE.

OF COURSE, WE EAT FERMENTED KIMCHI IN SPRING AS WE
DO THROUGHOUT THE YEAR, BUT A LOT OF THE KIMCHI
RECIPES WE MAKE IN SPRING ARE MORE LIKE SALADS:
SIMPLE PREPARATIONS TO BE EATEN IMMEDIATELY AS
WE ENJOY THE VIBRANCY OF THE SEASON.

DICED RADISH KIMCHI

Kkakdugi 깍두기

SERVES 10 AS A SIDE

Setting aside the ubiquitous cabbage, this is the most common kimchi enjoyed in Korea. It's cut into a distinct cube shape, which relates to the name – don't you think 'kkakdugi' sounds a bit like chopping? Radish can be made into all sorts of kimchi, but it's only called 'kkakdugi' if it's cubed.

2 daikon (white radishes)
2 tablespoons coarse sea salt

SEASONING
125 g (4½ oz/½ cup) Glutinous rice paste (page 21)
50 g (1¾ oz) gochugaru (Korean red chilli powder)
3 tablespoons aekjeot (fish sauce)
3 tablespoons Fermented fruit extract (page 20)
2 tablespoons minced garlic
1 tablespoon salted shrimp

Peel the skin of the radishes with a peeler, then dice into bite-sized cubes. Sprinkle the salt over the diced radish, then leave to soften for approximately 1 hour.

Quickly rinse the softened radish under cold running water (only wash the radish briefly to retain its sweetness), then drain.

Mix the seasoning ingredients together in a bowl.

Mix the radish with the seasoning in a container, then cover and leave at room temperature to ferment for 24 hours. Transfer to the fridge and continue to ferment for 1 week before eating. Kimchi keeps indefinitely, with some people preferring the sour, tangy flavour of well-aged kimchi and others preferring the fresher flavour of a shorter ferment – it's really up to you. Store in a sealed container in the fridge and remove each portion as you need it.

MUGWORT KIMCHI

Ssokgat kimchi 쑥갓김치

SERVES 2 AS A SIDE

In spring, kimchi tends to be more like a fresh salad, with less focus on fermentation and preserving, and more a sense of celebration of new life. So, it is here, using beautiful spring chrysanthemum greens, enjoying the bounty of the season.

200 g (7 oz) chrysanthemum greens, washed and cut into 4 cm (1½ in) lengths
½ bunch of chives, washed and cut into 4 cm (1½ in) lengths
½ teaspoon sesame seeds

SEASONING
3 tablespoons gochugaru (Korean red chilli powder)
1 tablespoon chilli flakes
1 tablespoon minced garlic
2 tablespoons salted shrimp
2 tablespoons Fermented fruit extract (page 20)

Mix the seasoning ingredients together in a bowl.

Add the prepared chrysanthemum and chives to the seasoning and mix thoroughly. Serve immediately with the sesame seeds sprinkled on top.

TIP
This kimchi is best served really fresh, so only make the amount you need on the day and serve immediately.

SPINACH KIMCHI

Sigeumchi kimchi 시금치 김치

SERVES 4 AS A SIDE

This is another salad kimchi, making the most of sweet, fresh spinach, which is left raw. Serve this spinach kimchi as a side dish with rice and a main course, preferably on the day it's made.

400 g (14 oz) English spinach
½ bunch of chives, cut into 4 cm (1½ in) lengths
50 g (1¾ oz) spring onions (scallions), trimmed and cut into 4 cm (1½ in) lengths
1 red cayenne chilli, destemmed and sliced
½ tablespoon ground sesame seeds

SEASONING
2 tablespoons aekjeot (fish sauce)
1 tablespoon salted shrimp
3 tablespoons gochugaru (Korean red chilli powder)
2 tablespoons Fermented fruit extract (page 20)
1 tablespoon minced garlic

Clean the spinach roots by scraping any dirt off with a knife. Cut the spinach in half lengthways and wash thoroughly, then strain through a sieve.

Mix the seasoning ingredients together in a bowl.

Add the chives, spring onion and chilli to the seasoning and mix well.

Add the spinach and mix gently, then sprinkle the ground sesame seeds on top to serve.

Spinach kimchi is best served on the day it is made, but if you do wish to store it, seal in an airtight container and refrigerate for up to 3 days.

PICKLED GARLIC SCAPES
Maneuljjong jangajji 마늘쫑 장아찌

SERVES 10 AS A SIDE

These pickled garlic scapes are a nice easy accompaniment to pull out of the fridge to enjoy as a side dish. This recipe is very mild but if you want to make it spicy, you can mix it with gochujang (Korean red chilli paste) or gochugaru (Korean red chilli powder).

300 g (10½ oz) garlic scapes, washed, dried and cut into 5 cm (2 in) lengths

PICKLE
200 ml (7 fl oz) Fermented fruit extract (page 20)
100 ml (3½ fl oz) All-purpose soy sauce (page 44)
100 ml (3½ fl oz) white vinegar
100 ml (3½ fl oz) cheongju or soju (clear rice wine)

Wash and dry the garlic scapes with paper towels to remove any moisture.

Place the garlic scapes in a sterilised 1 litre (34 fl oz/4 cup) glass jar.

Combine the pickle ingredients in a saucepan with 100 ml (3½ fl oz) water and bring to the boil over a high heat.

Once boiling, pour the pickling liquid over the garlic scapes.

Seal the jar and leave to sit at room temperature to pickle for 1 week. Once opened, the pickle will keep for up to 1 year in the fridge.

GOCHUJANG PICKLED GARLIC

Maneul gochujang jangajji 마늘 고추장 장아찌

SERVES 15 AS A SIDE

Garlic is revered in Korean cooking not only for its robust flavour but also for its medicinal properties. It's believed to boost the immune system and contribute to heart health, making it a natural fit in a cuisine that prioritises holistic well-being. One common method of incorporating garlic into Korean cooking is through pickling, and pickled garlic is used in numerous Korean condiments.

1 kg (2 lb 3 oz) garlic cloves, peeled
1 teaspoon sesame oil
1 teaspoon ground sesame seeds

PICKLE
(FIRST FERMENTATION)
750 ml (25½ fl oz/3 cups) white vinegar
60 g (2 oz) fine sea salt

GOCHUJANG JANGAJJI SAUCE (SECOND FERMENTATION)
500 g (1 lb 2 oz) gochujang (Korean red chilli paste)
125 g (4½ oz) gochugaru (Korean red chilli powder)
125 ml (4 fl oz/½ cup) Fermented fruit extract (page 20; see Tips)
125 ml (4 fl oz/½ cup) cheongju (clear rice wine) or soju
1 tablespoon fine sea salt

Wash and dry the garlic cloves with paper towel to remove any moisture.

Make a pickling liquid by combining the pickle ingredients with 500 ml (17 fl oz/2 cups) water in a container. Add the garlic, seal and leave to ferment in the fridge for 1 week.

After a week, strain the pickled garlic through a sieve, and let it sit on the sieve for 15 minutes to drain as much liquid as possible.

In the meantime, make the gochujang jangajji sauce by mixing the ingredients together in a bowl.

Add the drained garlic and mix well, then place in a container, seal and leave to ferment in a dry, shaded area for another week (see Tips).

Before serving, sprinkle the pickled garlic with the sesame oil and sesame seeds. Store in the fridge for up to 1 year.

TIPS
Use thick gochujang (Korean red chilli paste) for this recipe. If the paste becomes too watery after mixing with the garlic you can add more gochugaru (Korean red chilli powder) to thicken it up. Adjust the sweetness to your liking by adding more or less of the Fermented fruit extract.

PICKLED GREEN CHILLI WITH SOYBEAN PASTE

Gochu doenjang jang-ajji 고추 된장 장아찌

SERVES 15 AS A SIDE

Welcome to Yoora's favourite side dish! Luckily, it's easy and quick to make and keeps well in the fridge for a few weeks. You can serve this with anything to make the flavours more exciting but it's an especially good match with pork belly or other fatty meats.

1 kg (2 lb 3 oz) green chillies, rinsed, dried, destemmed and cut into bite-sized pieces
1 teaspoon ground sesame seeds

SEASONING
1 onion, finely minced
1 kg (2 lb 3 oz) Traditional Korean soybean paste (page 34)
100 g (3½ oz) minced spring onion (scallion)
125 ml (4 fl oz/½ cup) cheongju (clear rice wine), or soju
80 ml (2½ fl oz/⅓ cup) onion extract (see page 20)
250 ml (8½ fl oz/1 cup) Fermented fruit extract (page 20)
6 tablespoons gochugaru (Korean red chilli powder)
6 tablespoons minced garlic

Start by making the seasoning. Mix the onion with the soybean paste in a bowl.

Add the remaining seasoning ingredients and mix thoroughly.

Add the green chilli and stir to combine, then transfer to a sealed container and leave to ferment in the fridge for 24 hours.

To serve, scatter with the sesame seeds. This pickle will keep in the fridge for up to 1 year.

BRAISED BEEF & EGGS IN SOY SAUCE

Sogogi gaeran jang-jorim 소고기 계란 장조림

SERVES 20 AS A SIDE

1 kg (2 lb 3 oz) oyster blade
    (flat iron) beef
12 eggs

BEEF STOCK
1 onion, peeled
¼ daikon (white radish)
5 × 5 cm (2 × 2 in) piece of
    dried kelp
5 dried shiitake mushrooms
½ apple
125 ml (4 fl oz/½ cup) cheongju
    (clear rice wine) or soju
5 garlic cloves, peeled
1 cm (½ in) piece of ginger
1 spring onion (scallion), trimmed
    and cut into 3–4 cm
    (1¼–1½ in) pieces

SAUCE
1 litre (34 fl oz/4 cups) Beef stock
    (see above)
250 ml (8½ fl oz/1 cup) All-purpose
    soy sauce (page 44)
125 ml (4 fl oz/½ cup) Fermented
    fruit extract (page 20)
3 tablespoons honey or corn syrup
60 ml (2 fl oz/¼ cup) cheongju
    (clear rice wine) or soju
5 whole dried chillies, or to taste

This sweet and savoury dish immediately transports me back to my childhood. Create a quick, delicious bibimbap by combining your braised beef and eggs in soy sauce with hot steamed rice and a spoonful of butter.

Place the beef in a bowl of cold water and soak for at least 1 hour to remove the blood.

Place the beef in a pressure cooker and add the beef stock ingredients and 2 litres (68 fl oz/8 cups) water.

Boil the beef on high heat. Once the cooker whistles, leave it on high for another 5 minutes, then reduce it to medium heat for 20 minutes. Turn off the cooker and let the ingredients simmer in the residual heat for another 10 minutes. If you don't have a pressure cooker, place all the ingredients in a large pot and bring to the boil over a high heat. Once the broth boils, reduce the heat to medium, cover with a lid and cook for 2 hours, topping up the water as needed. Occasionally skim any fat that rises to the surface.

Bring the eggs to the boil in a saucepan of salted water and cook for 10 minutes, then drain, refill the saucepan with cold water and leave the eggs inside to cool. Once cooled, peel the eggs.

Drain the beef broth through a sieve into a clean saucepan and set the beef aside to cool. Once cool enough to handle, shred the beef with your hands.

Prepare the sauce by combining all the ingredients in a bowl.

Add the beef and eggs to the prepared sauce and bring to the boil over a high heat. Once the sauce boils, reduce the heat to medium and simmer for 30 minutes.

Taste the sauce and, once it is reduced to your liking, turn off the heat and leave to cool completely. Store it in the fridge and consume within a week. Remove the desired portion, and heat in the microwave for 2–3 minutes. Serve with rice and your favourite side dishes.

MARINATED EGGS IN SOY SAUCE
Gyeran jang 계란장

SERVES 6 AS A SIDE

This is an easy side dish of eggs pickled in a soy dressing. It keeps in the fridge for two weeks. All you need for a light meal is hot rice, one of these eggs and a few drops of sesame oil: mix it up and enjoy.

12 eggs

SAUCE
250 ml (8½ fl oz/1 cup) All-purpose soy sauce (page 44)
125 ml (4 fl oz/½ cup) Fermented fruit extract (page 20)
1 onion, chopped
30 g (1 oz/¼ cup) minced spring onion (scallion)
2 green chillies, destemmed and chopped
2 tablespoons minced garlic
1 teaspoon sesame seeds
1 tablespoon sesame oil

Bring the eggs to the boil in a saucepan of salted water over a high heat and cook for 10 minutes.

Transfer the eggs to a bowl of iced water and crack the shells gently with a spoon to allow the water to seep in (this will make them easier to peel). Refrigerate to cool completely.

Meanwhile, prepare the sauce by combining all the ingredients in a container.

Peel the eggs under running water and wash them well. Place the eggs in the prepared sauce and seal the container.

Store in the fridge and consume within 2 weeks.

WATER CELERY & BULGOGI HOT POT
Minari bulgogi jeongol 미나리 불고기 전골

SERVES 4

'Jeongol' means hot pot: this is a main dish that simmers away while you sit around and share it with a group. Initially, the broth may be a little bland but it becomes saltier as the soup boils down. Try to avoid having the broth too salty from the beginning.

There are all sorts of hot pots, but water celery, also known as dropwort, is a spring favourite and it's very good matched with soy-marinated beef.

Korean people love to finish a meal with rice. After you finish the meat and vegetables, you can make fried rice or porridge with the remaining soup. For porridge, boil cold rice and mix in an egg. For fried rice, retain 60 ml (2 fl oz/¼ cup) of the soup and stir-fry with a bowl of cold cooked rice, some finely chopped kimchi, some crushed roasted seaweed and sesame oil.

500 g (1 lb 2 oz) scotch
fillet (ribeye), cut into
2 mm (⅛ in) slices
100 g (3½ oz) shiitake mushrooms,
cut into bite-sized pieces
100 g (3½ oz) enoki mushrooms,
cut into bite-sized pieces
100 g (3½ oz) shimeji mushrooms,
cut into bite-sized pieces
30 g (1 oz/¼ cup) spring onion,
cut into 4 cm (1½ in) lengths
½ onion, sliced
1 red bullet chilli, destemmed
and chopped diagonally
200 g (7 oz) dangmyeon
(sweet potato noodles),
soaked according to the
packet instructions
200 g (7 oz) water celery
(dropwort), washed and cut
into 5 cm (2 in) lengths
150 g (5½ oz) medium-firm Tofu
(page 185), cut into
bite-sized pieces

BULGOGI SAUCE
125 ml (4 fl oz/½ cup) All-purpose
soy sauce (page 44), plus extra
to serve
125 ml (4 fl oz/½ cup) Fermented
fruit extract (page 20)
60 ml (2 fl oz/¼ cup) cheongju
(clear rice wine) or soju
½ nashi pear, peeled and cored
½ onion, peeled
3 garlic cloves, peeled
1 tablespoon sesame oil

HOT POT BROTH
5 × 5 cm (2 × 2 in) piece of
dried kelp
5 g (⅛ oz) dried anchovies
1 tablespoon dried shrimp
2 × 5 cm (2 in) slices daikon
(white radish)

Put all the ingredients for the bulgogi sauce in a blender and blitz until smooth.

Pour into a bowl, add the sliced beef, cover and place in the fridge for at least 1 hour to marinate.

In the meantime, make the hot pot broth. Place all the ingredients in a saucepan with 1 litre (34 fl oz/4 cups) water and bring to the boil over a high heat. Once boiling, reduce the heat to medium and simmer for another 10 minutes. Strain the broth through a sieve into a pot and discard the solids.

Place the marinated meat in the middle of a hot pot cooker or a large sauté pan with the mushrooms, spring onion, onion and chilli neatly arranged around the meat. Pour the broth in, bring to the boil over a high heat and cook for 10 minutes.

Reduce the heat to low, and check and adjust the seasoning. Add the dangmyeon, tofu and soy sauce to taste. Once the dangmyeon are cooked, add the water celery and cook for a further minute until the water celery has softened. Serve.

KOREAN KNIFE-CUT NOODLES
WITH FRESH PIPIS

Bajikrak kalguksu 바지락 칼국수

SERVES 2

This is a common spring noodle dish and very easy to make. It is typically prepared using Manila clams, which are easily found in South Korea especially during the spring season. That's why it's known as 'bajirak' (Manila clams) kalguksu. If you're having trouble finding Manila clams, pipis (vongole) or mussels make an excellent substitute. Kalguksu, which literally translates as 'knife-cut noodles', involves rolling out flour dough and roughly hand-cutting it into noodles. The type of broth used can vary from chicken to seafood, or even meat, depending on the region in Korea.

If you use fresh pipis, they may have sand in them. Make sure you purge them thoroughly by soaking them in salt water. There's nothing worse than sand in your mouth.

200 g (7 oz/1 ⅔ cups) plain (all-purpose) flour, plus extra for dusting
50 g (1¾ oz) potato starch
1 teaspoon fine sea salt

PIPIS
500 g (1 lb 2 oz) pipis (vongole)
1 tablespoon fine sea salt

VEGETABLES
5 garlic cloves, sliced
½ onion, sliced
1 tablespoon coarse sea salt
½ zucchini (courgette), julienned
1 red bullet chilli, destemmed and julienned

Make the noodles by mixing the flour, potato starch and salt with 130 ml (4½ fl oz) water in a bowl. Using your hands, bring the mixture together into a dough, then knead for 25 minutes, or until the dough stretches without breaking when pulled apart. Place the dough in a plastic bag and allow the gluten to rest for about an hour.

Briefly knead the dough on a lightly floured surface, then use a rolling pin to roll it out to a 2–3 mm (⅛ in) thickness, dusting with more flour as needed to prevent the dough from sticking.

Dust the bench with more flour and fold the dough in half. Dust the dough surface with flour and fold the dough in half again, then cut the dough into 5 mm (¼ in) lengths to create noodles.

To purge the pipis, put them in a bowl with 1 litre (34 fl oz/4 cups) water and the salt and refrigerate for 3 hours. Drain.

Place the pipis in a pot with the garlic and onion and cover with 2 litres (68 fl oz/8 cups) water. Boil over a high heat until the pipis open. Remove any that remain closed, then add the salt and 200 g (7 oz) of the noodles. Add the zucchini and chilli and bring back to the boil and cook for 3 minutes or until the vegetables and noodles are just cooked. Skim any foam that forms on the surface.

Taste and adjust the seasoning if needed. Transfer to a serving bowl and serve with kimchi.

1

2

3

4

5

6

Korean knife-cut noodles with fresh pipis (page 228)

SPICY BEEF SOUP
Yugaejang 육개장

SERVES 4

Koreans serve this chilli-rich red soup at funerals because the colour is believed to ward off evil spirits and bad luck. Also, beef is a luxury ingredient so it's a prestigious soup to serve to guests. Of course, these origins are mere folk tales that have lost their relevance in today's modern context. Nowadays, this dish has transformed into a go-to option for when you're craving satisfying, hearty and spicy comfort food. Serve with radish kimchi and rice for a perfect meal.

500 g (1 lb 2 oz) piece of beef brisket
1 tablespoon vegetable oil
½ tablespoon sesame oil
2 tablespoons gochugaru (Korean red chilli powder)
1½ tablespoons cheongju (clear rice wine) or soju
3 litres (101 fl oz/12 cups) Anchovy & kelp broth (page 19)
300 g (10½ oz) mung bean sprouts, washed and trimmed
50 g (1¾ oz) gosari (dried bracken; see Tip), boiled for 15 minutes until soft, then cut into bite-sized pieces
30 g (1 oz) spring onions (scallions), trimmed and cut into 5 cm (2 in) lengths
100 g (3½ oz) shiitake mushrooms, sliced

YUKGAEJANG SEASONING
½ tablespoon sesame oil
2 tablespoons gochugaru (Korean red chilli powder)
1 tablespoon minced garlic
50 ml (1¾ fl oz) Traditional Korean soup soy sauce (page 34)
½ tablespoon fine sea salt, or to taste
½ teaspoon ground black pepper, or to taste

Soak the beef in cold water for 2 hours to remove the blood.

Grease a pressure cooker with the sesame oil and vegetable oil and heat on medium.

Drain the beef, then sear on all sides for about 3 minutes, or until golden brown. Add the gochugaru and cheongju and sear for another 2 minutes.

Add the anchovy and kelp broth, seal the pressure cooker and cook on high until the pressure cooker whistles.

Once the cooker whistles, leave it on high for another 2 minutes, then reduce the heat to medium and cook for another 20 minutes. Turn off the cooker and leave the meat to simmer in the residual heat for about 10 minutes. Remove the beef and set aside to cool. Once cool enough to handle, shred the beef with your hands. Skim any fat from the surface off the broth and set aside.

For the yukgaejang seasoning, heat the sesame oil in a saucepan over a high heat and stir-fry the mung beans, gosari, spring onion and shiitake mushrooms with the gochugaru and garlic. When the vegetables soften, after about 5 minutes, add the shredded beef and broth and bring to the boil over a high heat. Once boiling, reduce the heat to low and simmer for 10 minutes. Add the soup soy sauce, salt and pepper to the soup.

Place the meat in a stone pot and add the hot soup and vegetables. Serve with kimchi and rice.

TIP
Called gosari in Korean, and sometimes known as fernbrake in English, these fern branches are dried and sold in packets. These are very stiff so make sure to soak in water for 6 hours to soften.

BRAISED SNAPPER

Domijjim 도미찜

SERVES 4

I've taken a traditional Korean fish dumpling and made it my own, tied up with a chive stem to make an elegant package of stuffed fish, preferably snapper, which is beautiful in spring. It's light, balanced, looks very elegant and always gets a great response when we serve it at CHAE.

400–500 g (14 oz–1 lb 2 oz) skin-on snapper fillet
½ tablespoon coarse sea salt
1 tablespoon makgeolli (cloudy rice wine)
100 g (3½ oz) mung bean sprouts, trimmed
4 chives
100 g (3½ oz) scotch fillet (ribeye), thinly sliced
1 shiitake mushroom, sliced

SAUCE
125 ml (4 fl oz/½ cup) All-purpose soy sauce (page 44)
125 ml (4 fl oz/½ cup) Traditional persimmon vinegar (page 55), or apple-cider vinegar
dried red chilli seeds, to taste (optional)

Cut the snapper fillet into four equal pieces.

Dip the snapper fllets in a mixture of makgeolli and salt, ensuring they are well coated. Cover and refrigerate to cure for about 3 hours.

Bring a saucepan of salted water to the boil over a high heat and blanch the bean sprouts and chives for 30 seconds, then drain and rinse under cold running water. Squeeze out any excess water with your hands.

Score the thickest part of the snapper pieces and open up the slits. Cut through the snapper pieces then open them out like a book to butterfly. Stuff the cavity with the bean sprouts, sliced beef and shiitake, and sprinkle in some salt. Fold the snapper back over the stuffing, then tie each parcel up with a chive.

Part-fill a large saucepan with water and place a colander or bamboo steamer basket on top, making sure the water doesn't touch the base of the colander. Place the pan over a medium heat and, once the water is simmering, steam the fish for about 10 minutes or until it is just cooked.

Meanwhile, make the sauce by mixing the soy sauce with the vinegar in a bowl.

Place the fish on a plate and sprinkle the sauce over the fish. Finish with some dried red chilli seeds if you like a little added spice.

1

2

3

COD IN MUSSEL BROTH
Daegu Jiri Tang 대구지리탕

Korean fish soup is usually spicy and red in colour thanks to all the chilli. This is my mild, pale version – 'jiri' means white and refers to both the fish and the broth. Given the delicacy of the flavours, you need a really good stock, made here with the sea-salty flavour of mussels. This soup is designed to be served from a pot in the centre of the table for everyone to share.

4 × 200 g (7 oz) skin-on cod fillets
½ tablespoon coarse sea salt, plus
  1 tablespoon for seasoning
500 g (1 lb 2 oz) mussels
¼ onion, sliced
1 tablespoon sliced garlic
2 whole dried chillies
90 g (3 oz) chrysanthemum
  greens, washed and sliced
  into 3 cm (1¼ in) lengths

SAUCE
2 tablespoons All-purpose soy
  sauce (page 44)
wasabi paste, to taste

Coat the cod fillets in the salt and leave to cure for 3–4 hours.

Prepare the mussels by scrubbing the shells with steel wool under cold running water and remove the beards.

Place the mussels in a pot and cover with water. Add the onion, garlic and dried chillies, cover and bring to the boil over a high heat. Once the soup boils, remove the lid and season with salt (be aware that mussel soup can overflow easily). Discard any mussels that haven't opened.

Place the salted cod pieces in the mussel soup and boil for 5–7 minutes.

While the cod is cooking, prepare the sauce by mixing the soy sauce and wasabi to taste in a bowl.

Once the cod is cooked, add the chrysanthemum greens and cook for another 1 minute. Remove from the heat and scoop into serving bowls with the sauce alongside for dipping.

BEAN SPROUT STEAMED RICE WITH SOY SAUCE DRESSING
Kongnamul bab 콩나물 밥

SERVES 4

This is a fantastic method to enhance a simple bowl of rice. By incorporating vegetables of your choice into the steamed rice, you infuse extra flavour, making your meal not only more delicious but also more nutritious. Bean sprouts and julienned radish are common choices for enhancing steamed rice, but feel free to get creative and test with your favourite vegetables to elevate your dining experience.

500 g (1 lb 2 oz) medium-grain white rice
200 g (7 oz/2 cups) soybean sprouts

SOY SAUCE DRESSING
100 ml (3½ fl oz) All-purpose soy sauce (page 44)
½ tablespoon minced garlic
100 g (3½ oz) chopped spring onion (scallion)
¼ onion, minced
1 teaspoon sesame oil
1 teaspoon sesame seeds

Place the rice in a pressure cooker and cover with cold water. Gently wash the rice, discarding the cloudy water. Repeat this process until the water runs clear.

Rinse the soybean sprouts under cold water. If desired, trim about 1 cm (½ in) from the ends of the sprouts for a more appealing presentation, and add them to the pressure cooker with the rice. Add 500 ml (17 fl oz/2 cups) water, cover with the lid and bring to the boil.

Once the cooker starts whistling, reduce the heat to medium and continue cooking for another 10 minutes.

After the rice and bean sprouts have finished cooking, turn off the heat and allow the pressure to release for about 10–15 minutes.

Carefully open the lid of the pressure cooker and use a spoon to fluff up the rice, separating the grains and bean sprouts.

Mix the dressing ingredients together in a bowl.

Serve a bowl of bean sprout steamed rice with the soy sauce dressing on the side, allowing diners to season their dish according to their preference.

SEASONAL SEASONED GREENS & VEGETABLES

Jaechul namul 제철나물

SERVES 2 AS A SIDE

The following three side dishes are made with seasonal vegetables and herbs, prepared with condiments that highlight their lovely spring flavours and freshness. The vegetables and herbs in Korea are different from those found in Australia but the ideas are adaptable. I would say the condiments are traditional but the hero ingredients are Australian in style.

SEASONED ZUCCHINI

Aehobak namul 애호박 나물

1 zucchini (courgette)
1 teaspoon fine sea salt
1 tablespoon vegetable oil
1 teaspoon minced garlic
1 tablespoon gochugaru
    (Korean red chilli powder)
1 tablespoon Traditional Korean
    soup soy sauce (page 34)
30 g (1 oz/¼ cup) chopped spring
    onion (scallion)
1 teaspoon sesame oil
1 teaspoon ground sesame seeds

Cut the zucchini in half lengthways and slice into half-moon shapes.

Place the slices in a bowl and scatter with the salt. Leave to sit for 10 minutes.

Heat the vegetable oil in a frying pan over a medium heat and stir-fry the minced garlic for about 30 seconds.

Add the salted zucchini, gochugaru and soup soy sauce and stir-fry over a medium–high heat for 3 minutes.

Once the zucchini is cooked, add the spring onion and sesame oil and cook for a further 1 minute until the spring onion is lightly cooked. Sprinkle over the sesame seeds to finish.

TIPS
If the zucchini is not thoroughly cooked, cover it with a lid and cook for another 1–2 minutes.

If the zucchini releases too much juice, stir-fry it over a high heat to evaporate the liquid.

SEASONED KALE

Kale namul 케일 나물

100 g (3½ oz) green kale, washed,
  hard stems trimmed

SEASONING
1 teaspoon minced garlic
1 tablespoon Fermented fruit
  extract (page 20)
2 teaspoons fine sea salt
1 teaspoon sesame oil
30 g (1 oz/¼ cup) finely chopped
  spring onion (scallion)
1 teaspoon ground sesame seeds,
  plus extra to serve (optional)

Cut the kale into bite-sized pieces.

Bring a saucepan of salted water to the boil and blanch the kale
for 30 seconds. Drain and immediately plunge the kale into a bowl
of cold water to stop the cooking process. Leave to cool.

Prepare the seasoning by combing all the ingredients in a bowl.

Drain the kale and squeeze out as much water as possible with
your hands. Place in a serving bowl, add the seasoning and mix
well. Place the kale on a plate and sprinkle over some more ground
sesame before serving, if desired.

SEASONED BOK CHOY WITH SOYBEAN PASTE

Bok choy doenjang muchim 청경채 된장무침

1 head bok choy

SEASONING
1 teaspoon minced garlic
1 tablespoon Traditional Korean
  soybean paste (page 34)
1 tablespoon Fermented fruit
  extract (page 20)
1 red bullet chilli, destemmed
  and minced
½ onion, minced
1 teaspoon sesame oil
30 g (1 oz/¼ cup) chopped spring
  onion (scallion)
1 teaspoon ground sesame seeds,
  plus extra to serve

Cut the bok choy into bite-sized pieces.

Bring a saucepan of water to the boil and blanch the bok choy
for 1 minute, then drain and immediately plunge the bok choy into
a bowl of cold water to stop the cooking process. Leave to cool.

Prepare the seasoning by combining all the ingredients in a bowl.

Drain the boy choy, then squeeze out as much water as possible
with your hands. Place in a serving bowl, add the prepared
seasoning and mix well. Sprinkle with some extra ground sesame
seed to serve.

FERMENTED RICE BEVERAGE
Sikhye 식혜

Sikhye is a traditional non-alcoholic beverage – the kind of drink everyone's grandma loves. The fermented flavours are delicious and there's texture from the floating rice pulp. Sikhye is also a base for rice syrup, so this is a foundation recipe for that, too.

When steeping the sikhye, it's important to use a low heat, otherwise the rice will disintegrate like a porridge instead of maintaining its firmness. If you have a Korean rice cooker or slow cooker, you can use the 'warm' function for gentle steeping.

225 g (8 oz) yeotgireum
(malted barley powder)
4 litres (135 fl oz/16 cups) water
250 g (9 oz) cooked glutinous rice
1 cm (½ in) piece of ginger
100 g (3½ oz) raw (demerara)
sugar, or to taste

Place the yeotgireum in a hemp fibre pouch and secure the opening with kitchen string.

Place the pouch in a large bowl and pour 1 litre (34 fl oz/4 cups) of water over it. Squeeze the pouch for 5 minutes, as if you are kneading dough or handwashing laundry. Transfer the cloudy malt water to a large pot. Repeat this process three more times, collecting a total of 4 litres (135 fl oz/16 cups) of malt water.

Add the glutinous rice to the malt water in the pot. Add the malted powder pouch, cover with a lid and let the ingredients steep for 5 hours over the lowest heat possible.

A small amount of rice will float to the top once the sikhye is well steeped, while most of it will remain at the bottom of the pot. Use a slotted spoon to remove the floating rice from the surface. Rinse it under cold running water and place it in a container to use as garnish when serving.

Strain the steeped sikhye through a fine-mesh sieve to separate the liquid from the rice that settled at the bottom. Pour the liquid into a large pot and discard the rice. Add the ginger and sugar and bring to the boil over a high heat.

Reduce the heat to low and simmer for another 10 minutes, then remove from the heat and leave to cool completely. Remove the ginger, taste and add some more sugar until it is sweetened to your liking. Transfer to the fridge to cool.

Garnish with the reserved rice pulp before serving cold.

NOTE
Yeotgireum is a barley malt powder with a sweet flavour. Made by allowing whole barley grain to sprout, it is an important ingredient for homemade gochujang and for sikhye. The enzyme amylase in barley malt powder converts the starch in rice into sugar at warm temperatures in water.

INDEX

A

acorn
    Acorn jelly 92
    Acorn jelly in broth 92
    Acorn powder 19
Adzuki bean porridge 181
Aekjeot (fish sauce) 19
All-purpose soy sauce 44
Anchovy & kelp broth 19

B

batter, Dry 120
Bean sprout side dish 137
Bean sprout steamed rice with
    soy sauce dressing 239
beef
    Braised beef & eggs in
        soy sauce 222
    Rice cake with beef spare
        rib soup 143
    Spicy beef soup 233
    Steamed beef 96
    Stir-fried beef gochujang 130
bibimbap 137
bingsu machine 24
Boiled pork, fresh kimchi &
    seasoned dried radish strips 195
bok choy with soybean paste,
    Seasoned 243
Braised beef & eggs in
    soy sauce 222
Braised mackerel 133
Braised snapper 234
broth
    Acorn jelly in broth 92
    Anchovy & kelp broth 19
    Cod in mussel broth 237
    Radish kimchi in chilled
        dashi broth 166
buckwheat noodles, Perilla oil 88
Bulgogi sauce 227

C

cabbage
    Cabbage kimchi 158–160
    Fresh napa kimchi 115
    Green cabbage & perilla leaf
        white kimchi 69
    Steamed beef 96
    Steamed napa cabbage with
        chilli oil 126
    White kimchi 162
cheongju 19
Chestnut rice stone bowl with
    seasonal herbs 137
chicken
    Chicken breast & cucumber
        salad 100
    Steamed chicken with crispy
        rice crust 198
chilli
    Chilli garlic sauce 126
    Crabs in spicy chilli sauce 174
    Glutinous rice red chilli paste 48
    Pickled green chilli with soybean
        paste 220
    Raw crab marinated in spicy
        chilli sauce & soy sauce 172
    Steamed napa cabbage with
        chilli oil 126
Chrysanthemum side dish 138
Cinnamon punch 103
Cod in mussel broth 237
Cold cucumber & seaweed
    soup 75
Cold eggplant soup 91
Cold soybean milk noodles 87
crab
    Crabs in soy sauce 175
    Crabs in spicy chilli sauce 174
    Raw crab marinated in spicy
        chilli sauce & soy sauce 172
cucumber
    Chicken breast & cucumber
        salad 100
    Cold cucumber & seaweed
        soup 75
    Pickled cucumber 76
    Stuffed cucumber kimchi 72

D

dehydrator 24
Diced radish kimchi 212
doughnut, Traditional Korean
    rice 151–2

dressing, Soy sauce 239
Dried radish greens in soybean
    paste 123
dried rice straw 24
Dried zucchini side dish 139
drink
    Cinnamon punch 103
    Fermented rice beverage 244
    Lemon, ginger & fermented
        sweetener tea 203
    Mandarin peel tea 202
    Pear ginger tea 144
Dry batter 120

E

egg
    Braised beef & eggs in
        soy sauce 222
    Marinated eggs in
        soy sauce 225
eggplant
    Cold eggplant soup 91
    Eggplant kimchi 66
    Fried eggplant 120
extract
    Fermented fruit extract 20
    Rice syrup extract 151

F

Fermented fruit extract 20
Fermented rice beverage 244
Fermented soybean stew 178
fermenter 24
fish
    Braised mackerel 133
    Braised snapper 234
    Cod in mussel broth 237
    Fishcake soup 129
    Monkfish fish ball soup 129
    Salted fish sauce 195
fish ball soup, Monkfish 129
Fresh napa kimchi 115
Fried eggplant 120
Frozen milk 148
fruit mesh bag 24

G

Gaeseong juak 151–2
garlic
    Chilli garlic sauce 126
    Gochujang pickled garlic 217
    Pickled garlic scapes 216
glutinous rice flour 20
Glutinous rice paste 21
Glutinous rice red chilli paste 48
gochugaru 20
gochujang 20
Gochujang jangajji sauce 217
Green cabbage & perilla leaf
    white kimchi 69
Ground soybean stew with
    pork 192
Gyeongdan (rice balls) 104

H

hemp fibre pouch 24
hot pot
    Tofu hot pot 188
    Water celery & bulgogi
        hot pot 226–7

J

jelly in broth, Acorn 92
jeotgal (Salted seafood) 21, 51
jocheong (rice syrup) 20
jujube 19

K

kale, Seasoned 243
kelp
    Anchovy & kelp broth 19
    dried, and other seaweed 19
kimchi
    Boiled pork, fresh kimchi &
        seasoned dried radish
        strips 195
    Cabbage kimchi 158–160
    Diced radish kimchi 212
    Eggplant kimchi 66
    Fresh napa kimchi 115
    Green cabbage & perilla leaf
        white kimchi 69

Kimchi pancakes 169–70
    Mugwort kimchi 213
    Nashi pear kimchi 110
    Perilla leaf kimchi 79
    Pomegranate kimchi 116
    Pork kimchi stew 134
    Radish kimchi in chilled dashi
        broth 166
    Sliced radish kimchi in brine 62
    Spinach kimchi 213
    Stuffed cucumber kimchi 72
    Traditional radish kimchi 114
    Watermelon rind kimchi 64
    White kimchi 162
Kimchi pancakes 169–70
Korean knife-cut noodles with
    fresh pipis 228
Korean rice wine 21

L

Lemon, ginger & fermented
    sweetener tea 203

M

mackerel, Braised 133
makgeolli 21
Mandarin peel tea 202
Marinated eggs in soy sauce 225
meju
    meju tray mould 24
    Traditional Korean soybean
        paste & soup soy sauce 34–7
melon
    Pickled melon 80
    Watermelon rind kimchi 64
milk
    Frozen milk 148
    Milk jam 104
mini greenhouse 24
Monkfish fish ball soup 129
Mugwort kimchi 213
mushroom
    Shiitake mushroom side
        dish 138
    Tofu, mushroom & perilla seed
        porridge 191
mussel broth, Cod in 237

N

Nashi pear kimchi 110
noodle
    Chicken breast & cucumber
        salad 100
    Cold soybean milk noodles 87
    Korean knife-cut noodles with
        fresh pipis 228
    Noodle seasoning 88
    Perilla oil buckwheat noodles 88

O

oil
    Chilli oil 126
    Perilla oil buckwheat noodles 88
    Steamed napa cabbage with
        chilli oil 126
onggi 24
Orange extract shaved ice 148

P

pancake
    Kimchi pancakes 169–70
    Potato pancakes with water
        celery 83
paste
    Dried radish greens in soybean
        paste 123
    Glutinous rice paste 21
    Glutinous rice red chilli paste 48
    Pickled green chilli with soybean
        paste 220
    Red bean paste 104–5
    Seafood soybean paste soup 99
    Seasoned bok choy with
        soybean paste 243
    Sticky fermented soybean
        paste 47
pear
    Nashi pear kimchi 110
    Pear ginger tea 144
    Pear pickle 148
    Steamed pear 201
perilla 21
    Green cabbage & perilla leaf
        white kimchi 69
    Perilla leaf kimchi 79

Perilla oil buckwheat noodles 88
Tofu, mushroom & perilla seed
    porridge 191
persimmon
    Traditional persimmon
        vinegar 55
pickle
    Pear pickle 148
    Pickled cucumber 76
    Pickled garlic scapes 216
    Pickled green chilli with soybean
        paste 220
    Pickled melon 80
pipis, Korean knife-cut noodles
    with fresh 228
Pomegranate kimchi 116
pork
    Boiled pork, fresh kimchi &
        seasoned dried radish
        strips 195
    Ground soybean stew with
        pork 192
    Pork kimchi stew 134
porridge
    Adzuki bean porridge 181
    Pumpkin porridge 182–3
    Tofu, mushroom & perilla seed
        porridge 191
Potato pancakes with water
    celery 83
Pumpkin porridge 182–3
punch, Cinnamon 103

R
radish
    Boiled pork, fresh kimchi &
        seasoned dried radish
        strips 195
    Diced radish kimchi 212
    Dried radish greens in soybean
        paste 123
    Radish kimchi in chilled dashi
        broth 166
    Seasoned dried radish strips 122
    Sliced radish kimchi in brine 62
    Traditional radish kimchi 114
    White diced radish kimchi 112
    White kimchi 162

Raw crab marinated in spicy chilli
    sauce & soy sauce 172
Red bean paste 104–5
Red bean shaved ice 104–5
rice
    Bean sprout steamed rice with
        soy sauce dressing 239
    Chestnut rice stone bowl with
        seasonal herbs 137
    Glutinous rice paste 21
    Glutinous rice red chilli paste 48
    Gyeongdan (rice balls) 104
    Rice cake with beef spare
        rib soup 143
    Rice syrup extract 151
    Saeal (sticky rice balls) 181, 182–3
    Steamed chicken with crispy
        rice crust 198
    Traditional Korean rice
        doughnut 151–2

S
Saeal (sticky rice balls) 181, 182–3
salad
    Chicken breast & cucumber
        salad 100
Salted seafood (jeotgal) 21, 51
sauce
    Aekjeot (fish sauce) 19
    All-purpose soy sauce 44
    Bulgogi sauce 227
    Chilli garlic sauce 126
    Crabs in spicy chilli sauce 174
    Gochujang jangajji sauce 217
    Salted fish sauce 195
    Simplified Korean soybean paste
        & soup soy sauce 40–2
    Ssamjang dipping sauce 195
    Traditional Korean soybean
        paste & soup soy sauce 34–7
seafood
    Cod in mussel broth 237
    Crabs in soy sauce 175
    Crabs in spicy chilli sauce 174
    Korean knife-cut noodles
        with fresh pipis 228

Raw crab marinated in spicy
    chilli sauce & soy sauce 172
Salted seafood (jeotgal) 21, 51
    Seafood soybean paste soup 99
Seasoned bok choy with soybean
    paste 243
Seasoned dried radish strips 122
Seasoned kale 243
Seasoned zucchini 242
seaweed
    Anchovy & kelp broth 19
    Cold cucumber & seaweed
        soup 75
    Radish kimchi in chilled dashi
        broth 166
    roasted 21
seedling heat pad 24
shaved ice
    Orange extract shaved ice 148
    Red bean shaved ice 104–5
Shiitake mushroom side dish 138
Simplified Korean soybean paste
    & soup soy sauce 40–2
Soju 21
soup
    Cold cucumber & seaweed
        soup 75
    Cold eggplant soup 91
    Fishcake soup 129
    Monkfish fish ball soup 129
    Rice cake with beef spare rib
        soup 143
    Seafood soybean paste soup 99
    Spicy beef soup 233
soybean
    Cold soybean milk noodles 87
    Dried radish greens in soybean
        paste 123
    Fermented soybean stew 178
    Ground soybean stew with
        pork 192
    Pickled green chilli with soybean
        paste 220
    Seafood soybean paste soup 99
    Seasoned bok choy with soybean
        paste 243
    Simplified Korean soybean paste
        & soup soy sauce 40–2

Soymilk 87
Sticky fermented soybean
    paste 47
Tofu 185
Traditional Korean soybean
    paste & soup soy sauce 34–7
Soymilk 87
soy sauce
    All-purpose soy sauce 44
    Bean sprout steamed rice with
        soy sauce dressing 239
    Braised beef & eggs in soy
        sauce 222
    Crabs in soy sauce 175
    Marinated eggs in soy
        sauce 225
    Raw crab marinated in spicy
        chilli sauce & soy sauce 172
    Simplified Korean soybean paste
        & soup soy sauce 40–2
    Soy sauce dressing 239
    Traditional Korean soybean
        paste & soup soy sauce 34–7
Spicy beef soup 233
spinach
    Spinach kimchi 213
    Spinach side dish 139
Ssamjang dipping sauce 195
Steamed beef 96
Steamed chicken with crispy
    rice crust 198
Steamed napa cabbage with
    chilli oil 126
Steamed pear 201
stew
    Fermented soybean stew 178
    Ground soybean stew with
        pork 192
    Pork kimchi stew 134
Sticky fermented soybean
    paste 47
Stir-fried beef gochujang 130
stone bowl with seasonal herbs,
    Chestnut rice 137
Stuffed cucumber kimchi 72
Suyuk spices 195

T
tea
    Lemon, ginger & fermented
        sweetener tea 203
    Mandarin peel tea 202
    Pear ginger tea 144
Tofu 185
    Tofu hot pot 188
    Tofu, mushroom & perilla seed
        porridge 191
Traditional Korean rice
    doughnut 151–2
Traditional Korean soybean paste
    & soup soy sauce 34–7
Traditional radish kimchi 114
Traditional persimmon vinegar 55

V
vinegar, Traditional persimmon 55

W
water celery
    Potato pancakes with water
        celery 83
    Water celery & bulgogi
        hot pot 226–7
Watermelon rind kimchi 64
White diced radish kimchi 112
White kimchi 162

Z
zucchini
    Dried zucchini side dish 139
    Seasoned zucchini 242

ACKNOWLEDGEMENTS

To Mom, for shipping countless boxes of fresh gochugaru, salt and all the local goodies from Korea.

To Yoora, for his creative direction and steering CHAE towards its unique identity.

To Pat Nourse, for discovering us.

To Gemima Cody, for putting us on the *Good Food Guide* map.

To Ellen Fraser, for showing us what it means to go viral.

To Shannon Martinez, for being my role model.

To Iain Ling, for helping us stay afloat during the rocky business transition.

To Michael Harry, for proposing the publication of our very first cookbook.

To Hardie Grant, for publishing our very first cookbook.

To Dani Valent, for translating our stories into beautifully written words.

To Armelle Habib and Lee Blaylock, for elegantly capturing the aesthetic of true Korean cuisine.

To Minhi Park, for the exquisite ceramics that embrace the beauty of Korean cuisine.

To the HG team, for their unwavering effort and incredible talent in bringing this book to life.

Most importantly,

To the thousands of people who have followed our journey as we shape CHAE into a unique brand. I wouldn't be where I am now if it wasn't for your support. I can't wait to share with you the exciting future for CHAE as we continue to work hard to introduce the authentic Korean flavour and culinary heritage.

Jung Eun Chae caused a sensation when she opened her tiny Brunswick apartment to six diners per night, four times a week, with a waiting list that exploded to more than 8000 people. She was named Gourmet Traveller's best new talent for 2021, and one of *The Age Good Food Guide*'s chefs of the year, thanks to her medicinal style of traditional South Korean cooking using from-scratch ferments and handmade sauces, enzymes, vinegars and kombuchas. CHAE was awarded two hats in the *Good Food Guide* for two consecutive years, in 2023 and 2024. She has since moved to semi-rural Cockatoo on the outskirts of Melbourne with husband Yoora and their labrador, where she continues to operate her six-seat restaurant.

Published in 2024 by Hardie Grant Books, an imprint of Hardie Grant Publishing

Hardie Grant Books (Melbourne)
Wurundjeri Country
Building 1, 658 Church Street
Richmond, Victoria 3121

Hardie Grant North America
2912 Telegraph Ave
Berkeley, California 94705

hardiegrant.com/books

Hardie Grant acknowledges the Traditional Owners of the Country on which we work, the Wurundjeri People of the Kulin Nation and the Gadigal People of the Eora Nation, and recognises their continuing connection to the land, waters and culture. We pay our respects to their Elders past and present.

A catalogue record for this book is available from the National Library of Australia

Chae
ISBN 978 1 74379 880 5
ISBN 978 1 76144 017 5 (ebook)

10 9 8 7 6 5 4 3 2 1

Publishers: Michael Harry, Simon Davis
Managing Editor: Loran McDougall
Editor: Andrea O'Connor, Asterisk & Octopus
Translator: Ashley Uhm
Design Manager: Kristin Thomas
Designer: Emily O'Neill
Cover illustration: Emily O'Neill
Photographer: Armelle Habib
Stylist: Lee Blaylock
Head of Production: Todd Rechner
Production Controller: Jessica Harvie

Colour reproduction by Splitting Image Colour Studio
Printed in China by Leo Paper Products LTD.

The paper this book is printed on is from FSC®-certified forests and other sources. FSC® promotes environmentally responsible, socially beneficial and economically viable management of the world's forests.